KEY ENGLISH TEST

Extra

WITHOUT ANSWERS

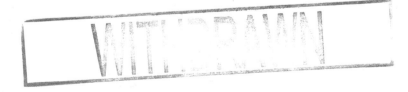

CAMBRIDGE
UNIVERSITY PRESS

CAMBRIDGE UNIVERSITY PRESS

Cambridge, New York, Melbourne, Madrid, Cape Town, Singapore, São Paulo, Delhi

Cambridge University Press
The Edinburgh Building, Cambridge CB2 8RU, UK

www.cambridge.org
Information on this title: www.cambridge.org/9780521714334

© Cambridge University Press 2008

It is normally necessary for written permission for copying to be obtained in advance from a publisher. The candidate answer sheets at the back of this book are designed to be copied and distributed in class. The normal requirements are waived here and it is not necessary to write to Cambridge University Press for permission for an individual teacher to make copies for use within his or her own classroom. Only those pages which carry the wording '© UCLES 2008 Photocopiable' may be copied.

First published 2008
Reprinted 2008

Printed in the United Kingdom at the University Press, Cambridge

A catalogue record for this publication is available from the British Library

ISBN 978-0-521-71434-1 Student's Book with answers and CD-ROM
ISBN 978-0-521-71433-4 Student's Book without answers
ISBN 978-0-521-71436-5 Audio CD
ISBN 978-0-521-71435-8 Self-study Pack

Contents

Acknowledgements

The publishers are grateful for permission to reproduce copyright material. It has not always been possible to identify the sources of all the material used, and in such cases the publishers would welcome information from the copyright owners.

For permission to reproduce photographs:
Corbis/Erin Ryan for p.16; Travelshots.com/Alamy for p.23; Corbis/Hulton-Deutsch Collection for p.26; Corbis/Yang Liu for p.32; Corbis/Christine Schneider for p.42; David Chapman/ Alamy for p.49; Corbis/Jon Hicks for p.50; Corbis/Martyn Goddard for p.68; Corbis/Jack Hollingsworth for p.74; Steve Bloom Images/Alamy for p.79; Corbis/David Butow for p.87; Corbis/Philip James Corwin for p.100; Corbis/Roy Morsch for p.104; Nikita Rogul. Image from BigStockPhoto.com for p.106; Corbis/ Phillipe Renault for p.108; PCL/Alamy for p.109; Corbis/ C. Devan for p.117; Daniel Cardiff/istockphoto.com, for p.126 (top left, top right) and pp.130 and 132; Nepal Images/Alamy for p.126 (bottom left, bottom right) and pp.134 and 136

Picture research by eMC Design Ltd www.emcdesign.org.uk

Cover design by David Lawton

The audio CD which accompanies this book was recorded at Studio AVP, London.

INTRODUCTION

Who is this book for?

Cambridge Key English Test Extra is for anyone preparing to take the Cambridge ESOL Key English Test (KET). It can be used at home or in class with a teacher.

What is in this book?

Cambridge Key English Test Extra includes four KET past papers from Cambridge ESOL. Each of the four tests includes a Reading and Writing test, a Listening test and a Speaking test. Before each part of each test, there are tips and exercises to help students prepare fully. There are also detailed notes giving information about KET, including what each paper consists of and how the exam is marked (see 'A Guide to KET' on page 6). The book is accompanied by an audio CD.

Cambridge Key English Test Extra is available in two editions: one with answers and one without. The 'With Answers' edition contains the answers to all the tasks and questions, including authentic sample answers for the Writing test, as well as complete recording scripts of the audio CD. It also includes a CD-ROM containing the same four Reading and Writing, and same four Listening tests that appear in the book, enabling students to practise for the computer-based KET. Both editions also contain specimen answer sheets which can be photocopied and used for practice.

How can I use this book?

Cambridge Key English Test Extra is organised by test paper. You can use the book in any order you wish. For example, if you would like to practise for the Listening test, you can go directly to that section in each test.

You should do the extra exercises that go with each part of each test before doing the actual tests themselves. These exercises highlight the problem areas of each test and give you suggestions on how to deal with them.

In the Reading and Writing tests, sample answers to the Writing components are supplied with the examiner's band scores in the 'With Answers' edition. Tips will advise you on how to improve your writing skills, telling you what you should and shouldn't do. You can then compare your answer with the sample answers.

You should always do the Listening tests without looking at the script. However, after you have finished the test, you can use the script to confirm what you have understood.

It is best to practise the Speaking test with a partner. However, the book gives you exercises to practise by yourself and tips to help you think about how to improve.

A GUIDE TO KET

The KET examination is part of a group of examinations developed by Cambridge ESOL called the Cambridge Main Suite. The Main Suite consists of five examinations which have similar characteristics, but are designed for different levels of English language ability. Within the five levels, KET is at Level A2 (Waystage) in the *Council of Europe's Common European Framework of Reference for Languages: Learning, Teaching, Assessment*. It has been accredited by the Qualifications and Curriculum Authority in the UK as an Entry Level 2 ESOL certificate in the National Qualifications Framework.

Examination	Council of Europe Framework Level	UK National Qualifications Framework Level
CPE Certificate of Proficiency in English	C2	3
CAE Certificate in Advanced English	C1	2
FCE First Certificate in English	B2	1
PET Preliminary English Test	B1	Entry 3
KET Key English Test	A2	Entry 2

KET is a popular exam with candidates who are learning English out of personal interest and for those who are studying for employment reasons. It is also useful preparation for higher level exams, such as PET (Preliminary English Test) and other Cambridge ESOL examinations.

KET is an excellent first step, helping you to build your confidence in English and measure your progress. If you can deal with everyday basic written and spoken communication (for example: read simple articles, understand signs and notices, write simple notes and emails), then this is the exam for you.

Topics

These are the topics used in the KET exam:

Clothes
Daily life
Entertainment and media
Food and drink
Health, medicine and exercise
Hobbies and leisure
House and home
Language

People
Personal feelings, opinions and experiences
Personal identification
Places and buildings
School and study
Services

Shopping
Social interaction
The natural world
Transport
Travel and holidays
Weather
Work and jobs

KET content: an overview

Paper	Name	Timing	Content	Test Focus
Paper 1	Reading/Writing	1 hour 10 minutes	Reading: Five parts which test a range of reading skills with a variety of texts, ranging from very short notices to longer continuous texts. Writing: Four parts which test basic writing skills.	Assessment of candidates' ability to understand the meaning of written English at word, phrase, sentence, paragraph and whole text level. Assessment of candidates' ability to produce simple written English, ranging from one-word answers to short pieces of continuous text.
Paper 2	Listening	30 minutes (including 8 minutes transfer time)	Five parts ranging from short exchanges to longer dialogues and monologues.	Assessment of candidates' ability to understand dialogues and monologues in both informal and neutral settings on a range of everyday topics.
Paper 3	Speaking	8–10 minutes per pair of candidates	Two parts: In Part 1, candidates interact with an examiner. In Part 2, they interact with another candidate.	Assessment of candidates' ability to ask and answer questions about themselves and about factual, non-personal information.

Paper 1: Reading and Writing

Paper format
The Reading component contains five parts. The Writing component contains four parts.

Number of questions
There is a total of 56 questions: 35 in Reading and 21 in Writing.

Sources
Authentic and adapted-authentic real-world notices, newspaper and magazine articles, simplified encyclopaedia entries.

Answering
Candidates indicate answers either by shading lozenges (Reading), or by writing answers (Writing) on an answer sheet.

Timing
1 hour 10 minutes.

Marks
Each item carries one mark, except for question 56 (Reading and Writing Part 9), which is marked out of 5. This gives a total of 60 marks, which is weighted to a final mark out of 50. This represents 50% of the total marks for the whole examination.

Preparing for the Reading component

To prepare for the Reading component, you should read the type of English used in everyday life; for example, short newspaper and magazine articles, advertisements, tourist brochures, instructions, recipes, etc. It is also a good idea to practise reading short communicative messages, including notes, emails and cards. Remember, you won't always need to understand every word to be able to do a task in the exam.

Before the exam, think about the time you need to do each part and check you know how to record your answers on the answer sheet (see page 138).

Reading			
Part	Task Type and Format	Task Focus	Number of Questions
1	Matching. Matching five prompt sentences to eight notices (plus one example).	Reading real-world notices for the main message.	5
2	Three-option multiple choice sentences. Six sentences (plus an integrated example) connected by topic or storyline.	Reading and identifying appropriate vocabulary.	5
3	Three-option multiple choice. Five discrete three-option multiple-choice items (plus an example) focusing on verbal exchange patterns. Matching. Five matching items (plus an integrated example) in a continuous dialogue, selecting from eight possible responses.	Understanding functional language. Reading and identifying the appropriate response.	10
4	Right/Wrong/Doesn't Say OR Three-option multiple choice. One long text or three short texts (maximum length 230 words) adapted from authentic newspaper and magazine articles. Seven three-option multiple-choice items or seven Right/Wrong/Doesn't Say items (plus an integrated example).	Reading for detailed understanding and main idea(s).	7
5	Multiple choice cloze. A text adapted from an original source, for example an encyclopaedia entry/ newspaper or magazine article. Eight three-option multiple-choice items (plus an integrated example).	Reading and identifying appropriate structural words (auxiliary verbs, modal verbs, determiners, pronouns, prepositions, conjunctions, etc.).	8

Preparing for the Writing component

To prepare for the Writing component, you should take the opportunity to write short messages in real-life situations, for example to your teacher or to other students. These can include invitations, arrangements for meetings, apologies for missing a class, notices about lost property, etc. They can be handwritten or sent as email.

Before the exam, think about the time you need to do each part and check you know how to record your answers on the answer sheet (see page 139).

Writing			
Part	**Task Type and Format**	**Task Focus**	**Number of Questions**
6	Word completion. Five dictionary-type sentences (plus an integrated example). Five words to identify and spell.	Reading and identifying appropriate vocabulary, and spelling.	5
7	Open cloze. Text type that candidates could be expected to write, for example a short letter or a postcard. Ten spaces to fill with one word (plus an integrated example) which must be spelled correctly.	Reading and identifying appropriate words with a focus on structure and/or vocabulary.	10
8	Information transfer. One or two short authentic texts (notes, adverts, etc.) to prompt completion of a text (form, notice, diary entry, etc.). Five spaces to fill with one or more words or numbers (plus an integrated example).	Reading and writing down appropriate words or numbers with a focus on content and accuracy.	5
9	Guided writing. Either a short text or rubric to respond to. Three points to communicate in writing.	Writing a short message, note or postcard of 25–35 words.	1

Part 6

This part is about vocabulary. You have to produce words and spell them correctly. The words will all be linked to the same topic, for example jobs or food. You have to read a definition for each one and complete the word. The first letter of each word is given to help you.

Part 7

This part is about grammar and vocabulary. You have to complete a short gapped text of the type you could be expected to write, for example a note and reply, or a short letter. You must spell all the missing words correctly.

Part 8

This part tests both reading and writing. You have to use the information in one or two short texts, for example a note, email or advertisement, to complete a document such as a form, notice, diary entry, etc. You will need to understand the vocabulary used on forms, for example *surname, date of birth*, etc. You will need to write only words or phrases in your answers, but you must spell and use capital letters correctly.

Part 9

You have to write a short message (25–35 words). You are told who you are writing to and why, and you must include three content points. To gain top marks, all three points must be included in your answer, so it is important to read the question carefully and plan what you are going to write. Before the exam, practise writing answers of the correct length. You will lose marks for writing fewer than 25 words, and it is not a good idea to write answers that are too long.

Mark Scheme for Writing Part 9

There are five marks for Part 9. Minor grammatical and spelling mistakes are acceptable but to get five marks you must write a clear message and include all three content points.

Mark	Criteria	
5	All three parts of the message clearly communicated. Only minor spelling errors or occasional grammatical errors.	
4	All three parts of the message communicated. Some errors in spelling, grammar and/or punctuation.	
3	All three parts of the message attempted. Expression may require interpretation by the reader.	Two parts of the message clearly communicated. Only minor spelling errors or occasional grammatical errors.
2	Only two parts of the message communicated. Some errors in spelling and grammar. The errors in expression may require patience and interpretation by the reader.	
1	Only one part of the message communicated.	
0	Question unattempted, or totally incomprehensible response.	

Paper 2: Listening

Paper format
This paper contains five parts.

Number of questions
25

Task types
Matching, multiple choice, gap-fill.

Sources
All texts are based on authentic situations, and each part is heard twice.

Answering
Candidates indicate answers either by shading lozenges (Parts 1–3), or by writing answers (Parts 4 and 5) on an answer sheet.

Timing
About 30 minutes, including 8 minutes to transfer answers.

Marking

Each item carries one mark. This gives a total of 25 marks, which represents 25% of the total marks for the examination.

Preparing for the Listening test

The best preparation for the Listening Test is to listen to authentic spoken English for your level. Apart from understanding spoken English in class, other sources include: films, TV, videos and DVDs, songs, the internet, clubs, and other speakers of English such as tourists, guides, friends and family.

You will hear the instructions for each task on the recording and see them on the exam paper. There are pauses in the recording to give you time to look at the questions and to write your answers. You should write your answers on the question paper as you listen. You will have eight minutes at the end of the test to transfer your answers to the answer sheet (see page 140). Make sure you know how to do this and that you check your answers carefully.

Part	Task Type and Format	Task Focus	Number of Questions
1	Three-option multiple choice. Short neutral or informal dialogues. Five discrete three-option multiple-choice items with visuals (plus an example).	Listening to identify key information (times, prices, days of week, numbers, etc.).	5
2	Matching. Longer informal dialogue. Five items (plus an integrated example) and eight options.	Listening to identify key information.	5
3	Three-option multiple choice. Informal or neutral dialogue. Five three-option multiple-choice items (plus an integrated example).	Taking the role of one of the speakers and listening to identify key information.	5
4	Gap-fill. Neutral or informal dialogue. Five gaps to fill with one or more words, or numbers (plus an integrated example). Recognisable spelling is accepted, except with very high-frequency words, e.g. 'bus', 'red', or if spelling is dictated.	Listening and writing down information (including spelling of names, places, etc. as dictated on recording).	5
5	Gap-fill. Neutral or informal monologue. Five gaps to fill with one or more words, or numbers (plus an integrated example). Recognisable spelling is accepted, except with very high-frequency words, e.g. 'bus', 'red', or if spelling is dictated.	Listening and writing down information (including spelling of names, places, etc. as dictated on recording).	5

Paper 3: Speaking

Paper format

This paper contains two parts. The standard format for Paper 3 is two candidates and two examiners. One examiner acts as an assessor and does not join in the conversation. The other is also an assessor (called the interlocutor) and he/she manages the conversation by asking questions and setting up the tasks (see Paper 3 frames on pages 125–129).

Task types

Short exchanges with the examiner and an interactive task involving both candidates.

Timing

8–10 minutes per pair of candidates.

Marks

Candidates are assessed on their performance throughout the test. There are a total of 25 marks in Paper 3, making 25% of the total score for the whole examination.

Preparing for the Speaking Test

Take every opportunity to practise your English with as many people as possible. Asking and answering questions in simple role plays provides useful practice. These role plays should focus on everyday language and situations and involve questions about daily activities and familiar experiences. It is also a good idea to practise exchanging information in role plays about things such as costs and opening times of, for example, a local sports centre.

Part	Task Type and Format	Task Focus	Timing
1	Each candidate interacts with the interlocutor. The interlocutor asks the candidates questions. The interlocutor follows a frame to guide the conversation, ensure standardisation and control level of input.	Language normally associated with meeting people for the first time, giving information of a factual, personal kind. Bio-data-type questions to respond to.	5–6 minutes
2	Candidates interact with each other. The interlocutor sets up the activity using a standardised rubric. Candidates ask and answer questions using prompt material.	Factual information of a non-personal kind related to daily life.	3–4 minutes

Assessment

You are assessed on your own individual performance and not in relation to the other candidate. Both examiners assess you – the assessor awards marks according to: Grammar and Vocabulary, Pronunciation and Interactive Communication. The interlocutor awards a mark for overall performance.

Grammar and Vocabulary

This refers to the candidate's ability to use vocabulary and structure. It also covers the ability to paraphrase to convey meaning.

Pronunciation

This refers to the intelligibility of speech. Having an accent from the candidate's first language is not penalised if it does not affect communication.

Interactive Communication

This refers to the candidate's ability to take part in the interaction appropriately. Hesitation while the candidate searches for language is expected and is not penalised so long as it does not strain the patience of the listener. Candidates are given credit for being able to ask for repetition or clarification if necessary.

Further information

The information in this practice book is designed to give an overview of KET. For a full description of all of the Cambridge Main Suite exams, including information about task types, testing focus and preparation, please see the relevant handbooks which can be obtained from Cambridge ESOL at the address below or from the website: www.CambridgeESOL.org.

University of Cambridge ESOL Examinations
1 Hills Road
Cambridge CB1 2EU
United Kingdom

Telephone: +44 1223 553355
Fax: +44 1223 460278
Email: ESOLHelpdesk@Cambridgeassessment.org.uk

TEST 1

Reading ● PART 1

TIP

Read the example and the notice that goes with it. Read the sentences numbered 1–5 and underline the important words.

Before you try to answer the questions in Part 1, read the example and the notice that goes with it carefully. Remember to cross out the example letter so you don't use it again by mistake!

Read sentences 1–5 and <u>underline</u> all the important words.

Now read the notices A–H and answer these questions.

Question 1

Which notices have telephone numbers in them?

Question 2

If you don't have cash, what else can you use to pay for something?

Question 3

Which notices have the words 'no' or 'not' in them?

Question 4

Which notices have an amount of money in them?

Question 5

What is another way of saying 'lower prices'?

Now answer questions 1–5 in Part 1.

PART 1

Which notice (A–H) says this (1–5)?
For questions 1–5, mark the correct letter A–H on your answer sheet.

Example:

0   You do not have to pay here.

Answer:

0	A	B	C	D	E	F	G	H
	☐	☐	☐	☐	■	☐	☐	☐

---

1   If you need a job, try telephoning this number.

A

> **JANE MUIR HAIRDRESSERS**
> *Appointments are not always needed.*

B

> We do not take traveller's cheques or credit cards.

2   You should pay with cash here.

C

> **FOUND!**
> Handbag with £50 cash
> See Sonia at reception

D

> CLEANER WANTED
> Will pay £6 per hour
> Call: 333456

3   Sometimes you don't have to book here.

E

> **CITY COLLEGE**
> **Free haircuts by student hairdressers**
> **Book on 017982**

4   If you find what this person is looking for, you will get some money.

F

> **VISIT CRYSTAL'S**
> *Our watches are the cheapest in town.*

G

> **Harry's Fruit Farm**
> Summer jobs for students
> Cash paid for all jobs

5   This shop has lower prices than the other shops near to it.

H

> **LOST!**
> **GOLD WATCH**
> **£50 for its safe return**
> **Phone 619342**

TIP

Read the instructions and look at the picture before you start. This will tell you the topic of the sentences.
Look at the words before and after the gap before you choose your answer.

The example and five sentences are about the same topic or they tell a short story. Before you start, look at the instructions and the picture.

Think about these questions:

1 What are the sentences about?

2 What is the picture of?

Before you choose the word that fits in the gap, look at the words before and after the gap. The word you choose from the A, B and C choice must fit with these. Think about these questions:

Question 6

Which word from the A, B, C choice fits with 'most' and 'sport'?

Question 7

Which word from the A, B, C choice fits with 'she' and 'about'?

Question 8

Which word from the A, B, C choice fits with 'Gloria' and 'on'?

Question 9

Which word from the A, B, C choice fits with 'she can' and 'some money from playing football'?

Question 10

Which word from the A, B, C choice fits with all the words before and after the gap?

Before you write your answers on the answer sheet read the sentences again with your answers filled in the gaps. Think carefully about the meaning of the sentences.

PART 2

QUESTIONS 6–10

Read the sentences about playing a sport.
Choose the best word (A, B or C) for each space.
For questions 6–10, mark A, B or C on your answer sheet.

Example:

0   Gloria .... playing sport very much.

    A   decides   **B**   wants   **C**   likes

Answer:

---

6   Gloria thinks football is the most .... sport she plays.

    A   favourite   **B**   interesting   **C**   nice

7   When Gloria plays, she .... about everything else and just thinks about football.

    A   leaves   **B**   forgets   **C**   loses

8   After school, Gloria .... on her football boots and plays with her friends.

    A   runs   **B**   changes   **C**   puts

9   When Gloria is older, she hopes that she can .... some money from playing football.

    A   earn   **B**   bring   **C**   take

10   One day Gloria wants to play football for her .... in the World Cup.

    A   country   **B**   nationality   **C**   group

TIP

Think about who is speaking, who they are speaking to, where they are and what they are doing.

Look at each of the five sentences numbered 11–15 (not the options A–C). Imagine you are the speaker.

Read these questions and answers for sentence 11:

• Who are you? (a person on the phone)

• Who are you speaking to? (the caller)

• Where are you? (at home)

• What are you doing? (answering the phone)

Answer the same questions for sentences 12–15.

Now choose the best answer, A, B or C, for questions 11–15.

PART 3

QUESTIONS 11–15

Complete the five conversations.
For questions 11–15, mark A, B or C on your answer sheet.

Example:
0

 How old are you?

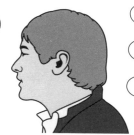

A Sixteen.

B Fine, thanks.

C How do you do?

Answer:

11	Hello. This is 245-6780.	A	I'll call again later.
		B	Thank you for your help.
		C	I'd like to speak to John, please.

12	I'm going to have a party on Saturday.	A	Who will come?
		B	Where to?
		C	How often is it?

13	What do I do at the traffic lights?	A	That's right.
		B	Turn left.
		C	You can't.

14	I'll take these grapes, please.	A	Can I help you?
		B	They're over there.
		C	Would you like a bag?

15	What colour will you paint the room?	A	I hope it was right.
		B	We can't decide.
		C	It wasn't very difficult.

Read the instructions and example only and answer these questions.

1 Who is speaking?

2 What is their relationship?

3 What are they talking about?

4 Which sentence, A–H, goes in the example gap?

5 Who does the car belong to?

First, read the sentences on the left, then the sentences A–H, and answer these questions:

1 Does Frank know how to drive the car?

2 Has Clare had lessons or taken a test?

3 What is Frank going to do now?

4 What does Frank invite Clare to do?

5 Who will be in the car with Frank and Clare?

Now answer questions 16–20.

QUESTIONS 16–20

Complete the conversation between two friends.
What does Frank say to Clare?
For questions 16–20, mark the correct letter A–H on your answer sheet.

Example:

Clare: Is this car yours, Frank?

Frank: **0** ....

Answer:

0	A	B	C	D	E	F	G	H
	▭	▭	▭	▭	▭	▭	▬	▭

Clare: Can you drive it?

Frank: **16** ....

Clare: Oh, I'd like to learn too, then I can get a car.

Frank: **17** ....

Clare: Lessons are expensive, and then there's insurance and petrol too. Mum says I can learn next year.

Frank: **18** ....

Clare: I'd love to. Where are you going to go?

Frank: **19** ....

Clare: But who's going to drive? It's dangerous if you are!

Frank: **20** ....

Clare: Okay, but please drive slowly.

A That's right. There are so many things to do.

B Don't worry. My dad will be there.

C Yes. We can both go.

D Well, why don't you?

E Not far, we'll be back in ten minutes.

F That's good. I'm going out in our car now. Do you want to come?

G It's not mine. It's Dad's.

H I can, but I need more practice.

Read the whole text first, before you read the questions. You do not have to understand every word in the text to answer the questions.

Read the text about the TV newsreader, Sean Murphy. This article is about the things Sean Murphy usually does in a working day. Some important words to know are the ones that tell us about time and what Sean Murphy does first and what he does next.

Look at the article again and <u>underline</u> all the words and phrases that tell you when and how often things happen in Sean's day.

Now look at questions 21–27.

Which questions ask about the different things that happen at different times in Sean's day?

<u>Underline</u> the words and phrases in those questions that ask you about when and how often things happen in Sean's day.

Now answer questions 21–27.

Remember, if you cannot find the information in the text, the answer is probably 'Doesn't say'.

PART 4

QUESTIONS 21–27

Read the article about Sean Murphy.
Are sentences 21–27 'Right' (A) or 'Wrong' (B)?
If there is not enough information to answer 'Right' (A) or 'Wrong' (B), choose 'Doesn't say' (C).
For questions 21–27, mark A, B or C on your answer sheet.

Sean Murphy

Sean Murphy reads the late news on British television at 11 o'clock each evening.

'This is a good time for a news programme because we can report the early news from America and the late news from Europe. I still arrive home before midnight because the journey from the Television Centre to my home in north London only takes six minutes. My family are all asleep when I get in, but I usually make a drink of hot milk and read a book for about an hour.

'I always get up to have breakfast with my three children before they catch the school bus. Then I take the newspapers and go back to bed for a short time. Later on, I go for a swim – newsreaders spend too much time sitting down! I sometimes go running. I've done the London Marathon twice. That's a race of over 40 kilometres. I finished each time, but I wasn't among the first!

'I start work after lunch at two o'clock, when I go to my office. The rest of the day is spent planning the programme, but I always try to go home for an hour to see my children before they go to bed.'

Example:

0 The late news begins at 11 o'clock every evening.

    A Right   **B** Wrong   **C** Doesn't say   *Answer:* | 0 | A ▬ | B ☐ | C ☐ |

----

21 Sean Murphy lives in London.

    A Right   **B** Wrong   **C** Doesn't say

22 Sean's wife gives him a hot drink when he arrives home after work.

    A Right   **B** Wrong   **C** Doesn't say

23 Sean takes his children to school in the morning.

    A Right   **B** Wrong   **C** Doesn't say

24 Sean likes to go swimming with his colleagues from work.

    A Right   **B** Wrong   **C** Doesn't say

25 Sean has won the London Marathon.

    A Right   **B** Wrong   **C** Doesn't say

26 Sean's working day begins in the afternoon.

    A Right   **B** Wrong   **C** Doesn't say

27 Sean usually leaves the office for an hour during the evening.

    A Right   **B** Wrong   **C** Doesn't say

Read the whole text first. Before you try to answer the questions, try to guess the word that goes in the gap.

Read the instructions, look at the title and picture, then read the text but do <u>not</u> look at questions 28–35.

When you read the article about London's Tower Bridge, think about what kind of word will go in each space. Can you guess some of the words?

Part 5 tests grammar. Before you do Part 5 for this test, answer the questions and look at the tips below.

Question 0

Which verb goes before 'visited' to make the present perfect tense?

Question 28

Remember, after the verb 'can' you use the infinitive form of a verb.

Question 29

Which adverb tells you the same machine being used today was also used in the past in 1894?

Question 30

Which adverb can go before 'busier' to make it stronger?

Question 31

Which modal verb can go in this space, before 'to open'?

Question 32

Which of these prepositions fit with the words 'was' and 'the middle'?

Question 33

This word tells us that the bus was on the bridge at the same time as it started to open.

Question 34

This sentence tells us how things are now.

Question 35

A bridge has two ends but in the text 'end' is singular. Which of the three adjectives, A, B or C, is the best word for this space?

Now answer questions 28–35.

QUESTIONS 28–35

Read the article about London's Tower Bridge.
Choose the best word (A, B or C) for each space.
For questions 28–35, mark A, B or C on your answer sheet.

London's Tower Bridge

Many tourists **(0)** .... visited Tower Bridge. It is the only bridge over the river Thames that can open and **(28)** .... ships pass under it. Tower Bridge was built in 1894 and **(29)** .... uses the same machines to lift up the two halves of the bridge. In earlier times, the river was **(30)** .... busier than now and the bridge **(31)** .... to open over a thousand times a year. Today, it only opens twice a week.

In 1952, a big red bus was **(32)** .... the middle of the bridge **(33)** .... it started to open. The driver only just got to the other side in time! Of course, now **(34)** .... are lights at **(35)** .... end and the traffic must wait for them to go green.

Example:

0	**A**	have	**B**	did	**C**	are	*Answer:*	0	A	B	C

28	**A**	lets	**B**	let	**C**	letting

29	**A**	ever	**B**	yet	**C**	still

30	**A**	much	**B**	too	**C**	very

31	**A**	should	**B**	had	**C**	was

32	**A**	to	**B**	between	**C**	in

33	**A**	because	**B**	when	**C**	if

34	**A**	there	**B**	here	**C**	they

35	**A**	every	**B**	each	**C**	all

TIP

All the words in this part are on the same topic. Think of all the words you know about the topic.

Read the first line of the instructions. It tells you the topic of all the words. In this test the words are 'holiday' words.

Before you answer questions 36–40, think of all the 'holiday' words you know. Put them in this table. The words already in the table are to help you get started.

Now answer questions 36–40.

How many of these words did you think of and put in the table before you answered the questions?

places	clothes	transport	things to take with you	things to do on holiday
hotel	sun hat	plane	luggage	swim
pool	swimsuit	car	ticket	read

PART 6

QUESTIONS 36–40

Read the descriptions of some holiday words.
What is the word for each one?
The first letter is already there. There is one space for each other letter in the word.
For questions 36–40, write the words on your answer sheet.

Example:

0   If you go on a camping holiday, you may sleep in this.   t _ _ _

Answer: | 0 | tent |

---

36   This is where you lie in the sun and go swimming.   b _ _ _ _

37   You can pack all your holiday clothes in this.   s _ _ _ _ _ _ _

38   Without this you cannot go to some countries.   p _ _ _ _ _ _

39   This is what you use to dry yourself after you go swimming.   t _ _ _ _

40   You need to put a stamp on this to send it to a friend.   p _ _ _ _ _ _ _

TIP

Read the text once, before you try to fill in the spaces, so that you understand what it is about. Remember to check your spellings.

Read the email.

Can you answer these questions about Heidi's email?

1 Where does Heidi's friend, Gabriella, come from?

2 What does Heidi need Gabriella to help her with?

3 Where di...

4 How many ... island of Sic...

5 How should G...

You need to unders... text before you try t... space.

Now answer questions ...

TIP

Read both ... 51–55. ... Loo...

PART 7

QUESTIONS 41–50

Complete the email.
Write ONE word for each space.
For questions 41–50, write the words on your answer sheet.

Example:

0	*from*

To:	Gabriella
From:	Heidi
Date:	?

Hi Gabriella,

You're **(0)** .... the island of Sicily, aren't you? I really need you **(41)** .... help me with my homework! I went to the library yesterday to **(42)** .... for a book because I need some information **(43)** .... Sicily. I couldn't find **(44)** .... good books there, just an old map! Can I ask you **(45)** .... few questions?

First, **(46)** .... big is the island? When did **(47)** .... become part of Italy? I **(48)** .... like to know one more thing. Farmers grow lemons there, but **(49)** .... they grow other fruit too?

Please email me your answers as **(50)** .... as possible!

Thanks,

Heidi

...exts before you answer questions
...hink about the topics of the texts.
...k at the spaces. Is the answer a number
...or a word?

Look at the job advertisement first and answer these questions.

1 What kind of people is the job for?

2 Where is the job?

3 How much money will they get for a day's work?

4 Which days of the week will they need to work?

5 If someone wants the job, what must they do next?

Now look at the note to Joan from Karen and find the following information.

6 the two jobs at the Forest Café

7 the pay per hour for each job

8 the number of hours for each job

9 the day of the week for each job

10 what Joan should do on Monday

11 the job Karen thinks Joan will prefer

Now do questions 51–55 and complete Joan's notes about the job.

PART 8

QUESTIONS 51–55

Read the job advertisement and the note.

Fill in the information in Joan's notes.

For questions 51–55, write the information on your answer sheet.

STUDENTS WANTED
for weekend work
up to £24 per day
Forest Café, telephone: **357550**

Joan – I've seen a job for you. The Forest Café needs a waitress. It's six hours' work on Saturday evening, starting at 7 pm. They pay £4 an hour. They need a cleaner too, for 3 hours on Sunday. But it's only £3.50 per hour and you won't like the work. Phone the manager on Monday at the café – or phone me on 354120 for more information.

Karen

Joan's Notes

Work at:	Forest Café
Job:	**51**
Day:	**52**
Number of hours:	**53**
Manager's phone no:	**54**
Money per hour:	**55**

TIP

Make sure you know who you must write to and why. Make some notes before you write your answer.

Read the notice and answer these questions.

1 Who is the notice from?

2 Who is the notice to?

3 What is the notice about?

4 How many questions are there in the notice? (Count the number of question marks.)

Remember you have to answer all the questions.

Now read Pedro's note below and answer the questions about it.

Hi Nick

I'd like to help with the concert. I like jazz and if you need hand, I can play the piano. I have a time this afternoon. Can I meet you at 1.30 at school hall?

Bye

Pedro

5 Does Pedro write his note to the right person?

6 Does Pedro answer all the questions? <u>Underline</u> his answers.

7 What does Pedro write to show his note is finished?

8 Can you see any grammar mistakes in Pedro's note? What are they?

9 You can get 5 marks for this part of the test. How many marks do you think Pedro got for this note?

Now read this note and answer the questions below.

Helo Students

What music I like is disco. What can I do to help with concert? When you free to come to meeting about concert?

10 Is the note written to the right person?

11 Are all the questions answered?

12 Is it clear who this note was written by?

13 Do you think this note got the full 5 marks?

Now write your note to Nick.

PART 9

QUESTION 56

You have seen this notice in your school.

> ## ALL STUDENTS:
>
> We are going to do a concert at school.
>
> What music do you like?
> What can you do to help with the concert?
> When are you free to come to
> a meeting about the concert?
>
> Nick (Class 5)

You want to help with the concert.

Write a note to Nick and answer the questions.

Write 25–35 words.

Write the note on your answer sheet.

Listening • PART 1

TIP

Look at each of the questions and pictures and think about what words you need to listen for.

There are five questions in Part 1. You will see that, here, each question has three pictures after it, pictures A, B and C.

Before you listen to the recording, look at each question and the pictures and fill in this table.

Question 1 has been filled in for you.

Question 1
Which words do you think you may hear?
weather, cloud/cloudy, rain/raining/rained, storm, sunny/sunshine/sun, warm, hot, wet, cold, sky

Question 2
Which words do you think you may hear?

Question 3
Which words do you think you may hear?

Question 4
Which words do you think you may hear?

Question 5
Which words do you think you may hear?

Now listen to the recording and answer questions 1–5.

Did you hear any of the words you put into the table?

Did you hear any words you did not put in your table?

Listen again and add the words you hear to the table.

PART 1

QUESTIONS 1–5

You will hear five short conversations.
You will hear each conversation twice.
There is one question for each conversation.
For questions 1–5, put a tick (✓) under the right answer.

Example:

0   How many people were at the meeting?

3	**13**	**30**
A ☐	B ☐	C ✓

1 What was the weather like when the holiday began?

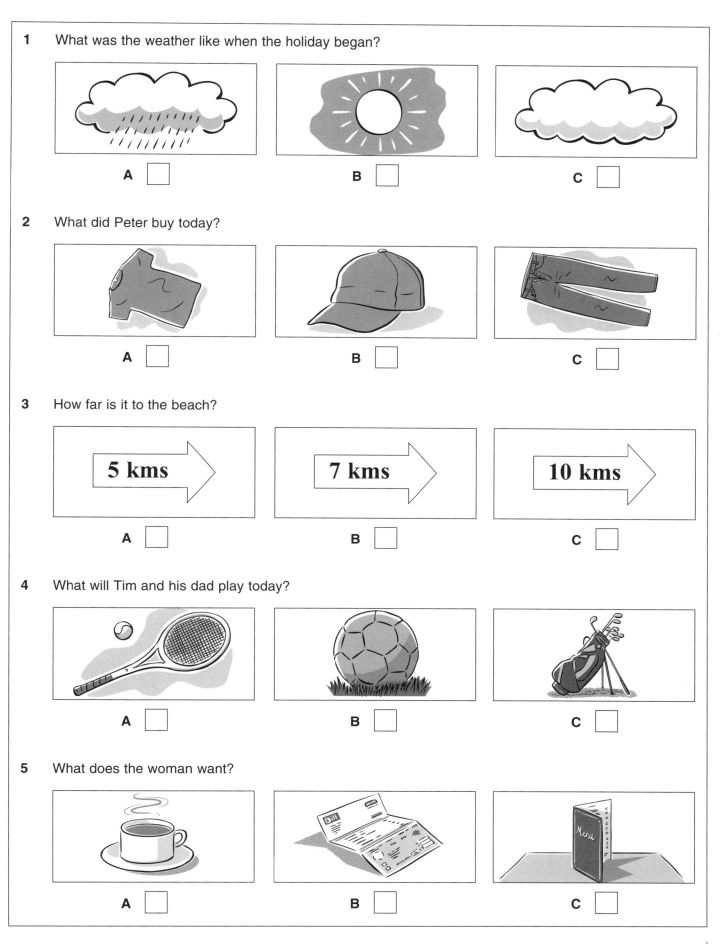

A ☐   B ☐   C ☐

2 What did Peter buy today?

A ☐   B ☐   C ☐

3 How far is it to the beach?

5 kms ➡   **7 kms** ➡   **10 kms** ➡

A ☐   B ☐   C ☐

4 What will Tim and his dad play today?

A ☐   B ☐   C ☐

5 What does the woman want?

A ☐   B ☐   C ☐

TIP

The information in the conversation you hear will be in the same order as questions 6–10. Before you listen, make sure you read the questions and answers carefully.

Look at the instructions, read them as you listen to them on the recording. Then stop the recording.

Read these questions before you listen to the recording, then answer them.

1 Who is talking?

2 Who has to do the things on the right of the page, A–H?

3 What will happen at 11 o'clock?

To help you find your way through the listening, you will have to listen for the times.

Listen to the recording and write down all the times you hear. Pay attention to which time is mentioned first, second, etc.

Now look at the list of 'things to do' on the right then listen to the recording again and answer questions 6–10.

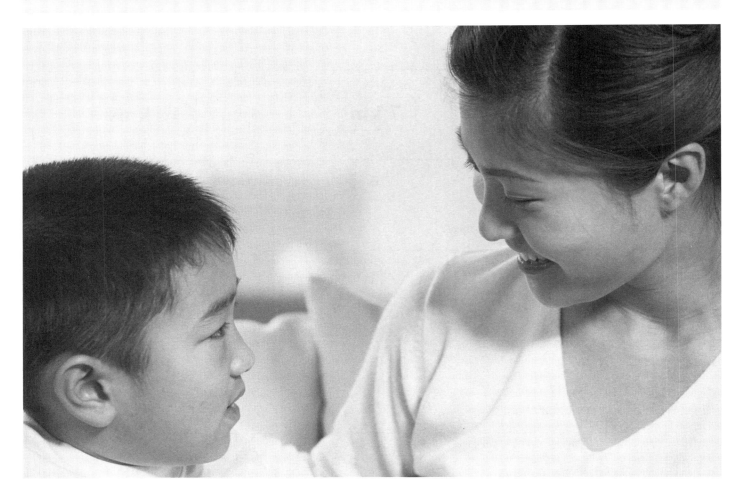

PART 2

QUESTIONS 6–10

Listen to a woman talking to her son, Chris, about the things he has to do.
What will he do at each time?
For questions 6–10, write a letter A–H next to each time.
You will hear the conversation twice.

Example:

0   11.00 |E|

Times		**Things to do**	
6	12.00 ☐	**A**	buy stamps
		B	drive to pool
7	12.30 ☐	**C**	go to library
8	1.00 ☐	**D**	have lunch
		E	phone grandparents
9	1.30 ☐	**F**	visit friends
		G	wash car
10	2.00 ☐	**H**	watch TV

TIP

Read the instructions and questions before you listen. They can tell you a lot about what you will hear.

Look at the instructions, example and the five questions, 11–15.

In the test you will have 20 seconds to do this, so try to do it that fast now. <u>Underline</u> **any important words.**

Now answer these questions.

1   Who is talking about a birthday party?
2   How many people will be at the party?
3   What kind of food do they talk about?
4   Is it Amanda's birthday?
5   Will the party be in the afternoon?

When you hear the recording, you will be listening for certain information.

The points below will help you.

Question 11

You will hear all three words, 'coffee', 'lemon' and 'apple', but only one of them will be about the ice cream. The other two will be about other types of food.

Question 12

All three of these can be used to play music at the party, but only one of them is broken. Can you think of another way to say 'broken'?

Question 13

You may hear all three names, so listen carefully. Remember, the correct answers will all come from the woman, Amanda, not the man.

Question 14

You will hear all three words, 'camera', 'video' and 'football', but only one will be the present Amanda bought. Listen for negatives; words like 'didn't', 'couldn't', 'won't', etc. They might tell you what she didn't buy.

Question 15

You will hear all three times but other things will be happening at those times. Listen for another way of saying 'arrive'.

Now listen to the recording and answer questions 11–15.

PART 3

QUESTIONS 11–15

Listen to Amanda talking to a friend about a birthday party.
For questions 11–15, tick (✓) A, B or C.
You will hear the conversation twice.

Example:

0	How many people can come to the party?	A	8	☐
		B	11	✓
		C	18	☐

11	Which ice cream will they have at the party?	A	coffee	☐
		B	lemon	☐
		C	apple	☐

12	What is broken?	A	the CD player	☐
		B	the cassette recorder	☐
		C	the guitar	☐

13	Whose birthday is it?	A	Emma's	☐
		B	Joan's	☐
		C	Amanda's sister's	☐

14	What present has Amanda bought?	A	a camera	☐
		B	a video	☐
		C	a football	☐

15	What time should people arrive at the party?	A	8 p.m.	☐
		B	8.30 p.m.	☐
		C	9.30 p.m.	☐

Read the instructions and the notes before you listen, so that you know what kind of words you have to write.

In this part of the test you have to write down information on a form or in some notes.

Look at the instructions and notes and decide what kind of information you will need to listen for. Match the questions with the kind of information you will need to write. There are two kinds of information that you do **not** need. The first one has been done for you.

Question 16 ⟩ a day of the week
Question 17 ⟩ time
　　　　　　something you wear
Question 18　price or amount of money
Question 19　a spelling of a name
Question 20　a word
　　　　　　a number

When you hear the recording, you will not always hear the prompt words that are already on the notes.

For example, for question 16 the woman has written 'to sell' on the notes but you may not hear 'the job is to sell …' in the recording. The man will say it in a different way.

For example:　The job is selling …
You will be selling …
The job is in the … department
You will work in the … department, selling …

Can you think of different ways of saying these sentences?

1　You begin work at … a.m.
2　You will work on these days: Tuesday to …
3　Your pay will be £ … per hour.
4　You write to Mrs …

Now listen to the recording and answer questions 16–20.

PART 4

QUESTIONS 16–20

You will hear a woman asking for some information about a job.
Listen and complete questions 16–20.
You will hear the conversation twice.

JOB

At:　Jones Department Store

To sell:　**16**

Begin work at:　**17** …………………………………… a.m.

Days:　**18** Tuesday to ……………………………

Pay:　**19** £ ………………………… per hour

Write to:　**20** Mrs ……………………………

Remember, write your answers on the question paper first. You will have time to write your answers on the answer sheet at the end of the test.

Some students worry about listening and writing at the same time.

If you quickly write the answers onto the question paper first, you will have enough time to copy them onto the answer sheet later. Remember to check your spellings.

Before you listen, look at the instructions and notes about a town called Langley.

Match the questions with the kind of information you need to answer the questions. The first one has been done for you. There are two kinds of information that you do not need.

Question 21 — a telephone number
Question 22 — the price of something
Question 23 — a name
Question 24 — a time
Question 25 — something in the Town Hall
a date
a place

Now listen to the recording and write the answers to questions 21–25 in the boxes on the question paper.

Did you have enough time to write and listen?

If you have problems and miss one answer, don't worry. Start to listen for the next answer. You can try to answer the question you missed when you listen for the second time.

PART 5

QUESTIONS 21–25

You will hear some tourist information about a town called Langley.
Listen and complete questions 21–25.
You will hear the information twice.

Langley

Tourists stop here for:		3 hours
Town Hall		
See the:	**21**	
Cost of ticket:	**22**	.... pence
Langley Park		
Café is near:	**23**	
Tour of town		
Meet guide in:	**24**	.... street
Leave Langley at:	**25**	.... p.m.

You now have 8 minutes to write your answers on the answer sheet.

The Speaking test lasts 8 to 10 minutes. You will take the test with another candidate. There are two examiners, but only one of them will talk to you. The examiner will ask you questions and ask you to talk to the other candidate.

Part 1 (5–6 minutes)
The examiner will ask you and your partner some questions. These questions will be about your daily life, past experience and future plans. For example, you may have to speak about your school, job, hobbies or home town.

Part 2 (3–4 minutes)
You and your partner will speak to each other. You will ask and answer questions. The examiner will give you a booklet with some information in it. The examiner will give your partner a booklet with some words in it. Your partner will use the words in the booklet to ask you questions about the information you have. Then you will change roles.

Speaking ● PART 1

TIP

Practise talking about yourself and your likes and dislikes.

In the first part of the test the examiner will ask you questions about yourself.

Below are some examples of the kind of questions the examiner will ask you.

Read the questions and try to answer them.

Remember to say the answers; do not write them down – this is a speaking test.

1 What's your name?
2 How do you spell your surname (family name)?
3 Are you a student?
4 What do you do/study?
5 Do you like your job? Why (not)?
6 Where are you from?
7 How long have you lived here?
8 Tell me about your house or flat.
9 What music do you like?
10 Can you play the piano?
11 Tell me about your favourite CD.

Try to give more than a one-word answer.

Question 3 can be answered with just a 'yes' or 'no', and you can answer question 4 with just one word, e.g., 'What do you study?' – 'maths.'

Always try to say more than just one word. Put the word into a sentence.

For example:

Question	Answer
Are you a student?	Yes, I study at the city college.
What do you study?	I study maths. It's my favourite subject.

TIP

Look at your partner when you ask and answer questions.

In the second part of the test you talk to your partner, so remember to look at them when you are talking.

The examiner will first give you and your partner some information about a bird park. Look on pages 130 and 132 for the information (1A) and the prompt questions (1B) for the bird park.

The examiner will tell you what you have to do. Before you start, take a little time to read the information and prompt questions the examiner gives to you. When you have finished reading, you can look up at your partner and smile, to show that you are ready to start.

Look at the prompt questions 1B on page 132. Try asking five questions about the bird park. Remember to just say them, not write them down.

When you are sure you have five good questions, look at the information 1A on page 130 and try to find the answers to your questions.

If possible, practise this part of the test with another student.

There is a task (1C and 1D) about an elephant ride on pages 134 and 136. Use this for some practice.

When you ask and answer questions together, remember to look at your partner. Smile and be friendly.

TEST 2

Reading ● PART 1

TIP

Think about where you could see each notice and who it is for.

Before you answer questions 1–5, read notices A–H and think about where you could see them and who they are for.

Notice A

1 Where could you see this notice?
  a in a newspaper
  b on a car
  c beside a telephone

2 Who is it for?
  a someone who wants to make a phone call
  b someone who is a manager
  c someone who wants a job in a garage

Notice B

1 Where could you see this notice?
  a in a taxi
  b on a road
  c at a train station

2 Who is it for?
  a train drivers
  b people walking
  c car drivers

Notice C

1 Where could you see this notice?
  a in a sports centre
  b in a clothes shop
  c in a jeans factory

2 Who is it for?
  a people trying on clothes
  b people wearing jeans
  c someone called Jane

Notice D

1 Where could you see this notice?
  a in a house
  b on a fridge
  c in a café

2 Who is it for?
  a a waiter
  b a customer
  c a cleaner

Notice E

1 Where could you see this notice?
  a in a newspaper
  b in a telephone book
  c in a kitchen

2 Who is it for?
  a someone who needs help
  b someone who likes cooking
  c someone who wants to help

Notice F

1 Where could you see this notice?
  a at Cambridge station
  b on a train
  c in a newspaper

2 Who is it for?
  a people going to Cambridge
  b people from Stevenage
  c people working on a train

Notice G

1 Where could you see this notice?
  a on a new shirt
  b in Saturday's newspaper
  c in a shop window

2 Who is it for?
  a people who wash clothes
  b people who want their clothes cleaned
  c people who want to buy clothes today

Notice H

1 Where could you see this notice?
  a on a cook book
  b on a restaurant menu
  c on a noticeboard

2 Who is it for?
  a people who want to learn to cook
  b people learning Chinese
  c cookery teachers

Now answer questions 1–5.

PART 1

QUESTIONS 1–5

Which notice (A–H) says this (1–5)?
For questions 1–5, mark the correct letter A–H on your answer sheet.

Example:

0   You can get something to eat here.

Answer:

0	A	B	C	D	E	F	G	H
	▢	▢	▢	▬	▢	▢	▢	▢

----

1   You can learn how to make different kinds of food on this course.

A
Mechanic needed
Call garage Manager
(Cambridge 221507)

B
**Cambridge Station
taxi drivers only**

2   You have to get off one train and get on another if you want to go to Cambridge.

C
Jane's Jeans
No more than 3 pairs
in the changing room

D
*Try our home-made
hot and cold snacks*

3   Phone this person if you want a job working with cars.

E
For help with cooking
and housework
telephone Carol on 332768

4   If you want someone to wash some clothes for you, it will be cheaper this week.

F
**Passengers for Cambridge
change at Stevenage Station**

G
**Clean shirts in 24 hours
Half-price until Saturday**

5   You mustn't take too many clothes to try on.

H
Chinese and Thai
cooking lessons
start here on Saturday

TIP

Try to think of the word for each space before you look at the words A–C.

Read sentences 0 and 6–10 but don't look at the words A, B or C below each sentence. Put your hand over them so you can't see them. Think about the meaning of each sentence.

Now read each sentence again.

What is the word in each gap (questions 0 and 6–10)? Choose from the list below.

    a noun

    a verb

    an adjective

    an adverb

Think about these questions but remember not to look at the A, B or C options.

Question 0

What did Sarah Packer do for the first time on Monday?

Question 6

What is Sarah doing for four years at university?

Question 7

What did the university secretary do to all the new students?

Question 8

What did Sarah and her new teachers do on the first day?

Question 9

How does Sarah feel today?

Question 10

What is Sarah going to do next month?

Now answer questions 6–10.

PART 2

QUESTIONS 6–10

Read the sentences about a university student.
Choose the best word (A, B or C) for each space.
For questions 6–10, mark A, B or C on your answer sheet.

Example:

0   Sarah Packer .... to university for the first time on Monday.

    A arrived   **B** went   **C** was

Answer:

0	A	B	C
	▭	▬	▭

---

6   Sarah is doing a four-year .... in Business Studies.

    A class   **B** lesson   **C** course

7   The university secretary was there to .... all the new students.

    A invite   **B** speak   **C** welcome

8   On the first day, Sarah .... some of her new teachers.

    A met   **B** knew   **C** remembered

9   Today, Sarah is .... reading her business books.

    A correct   **B** useful   **C** busy

10   Next month, Sarah is hoping to .... the university swimming club.

    A play   **B** join   **C** become

TIP

Before you look at the A, B, C options, read each sentence and think about what you would say in each situation.

Before you look at questions 11–15, read the five situations below and think about what you would say.

1 You are at home, the phone rings and your mother asks you to answer it. You don't want to because you are busy.

2 Your friend asks you if you want to drink lemonade or orange juice. You don't want either and would prefer a different drink.

3 You are standing on a station platform waiting for the 9.15 train to take you to college, like you do every day. Someone tells you the train is late. It has been late every day this week.

4 You are sitting at home with your friend from school, doing your homework. She is having problems with her homework and asks you for help. You are having problems with it too.

5 You have just seen a play and are walking out of a theatre with a friend. He says the play was boring. You don't agree.

Now read questions 11–15 and choose the best answer, A, B or C, for each one.

PART 3

QUESTIONS 11–15

Complete the five conversations.
For questions 11–15, mark A, B or C on your answer sheet.
Example:
0

 *Where do you come from?*

A New York.
B School.
C Home.

Answer:

0	A	B	C
	▬	☐	☐

---

11 Please answer the phone.

    A How are you?
    B Why can't you?
    C When did he call?

12 Would you prefer lemonade or orange juice?

    A Have you got anything else?
    B If you like.
    C Are you sure about that?

13 The 9.15 train's late again.

    A It was never there.
    B It often is.
    C Will it ever be?

14 Can you help me with my homework?

    A I don't understand it.
    B It's not ready.
    C I can't help it.

15 I thought the play was very boring.

    A Yes, I'd like to.
    B Which did you think?
    C I enjoyed it.

TIP

Imagine you are the second speaker. Do not read sentences A–H. Just read what the first speaker says and think about what you reply.

To help you understand the conversation, read the instructions and what Mrs Brown says. Think about the questions below. Do not read sentences A–H.

1   Have Jack and Mrs Brown met before?

2   Why is Jack talking to Mrs Brown?

3   What does Mrs Brown ask Jack?

4   What do you think Jack asks Mrs Brown about in spaces 17, 19 and 20?

5   What does Mrs Brown say is close to the house?

Now imagine that you are Jack and think about what you would say in each of the spaces, 16–20.

Now read the sentences A–H and answer questions 16–20.

QUESTIONS 16–20

Complete the conversation about renting a room.
What does Jack say to Mrs Brown?
For questions 16–20, mark the correct letter A–H on your answer sheet.

Example:

Mrs Brown: Good morning. Are you Jack Gomez?

Jack: **0** ....

Answer:

0	A	B	C	D	E	F	G	H
	▢	▢	▢	▢	▢	▢	▬	▢

Mrs Brown: Come this way. Here it is.

Jack: **16** ....

Mrs Brown: And it's very warm. The rent is £400 a month.

Jack: **17** ....

Mrs Brown: There's nothing more to pay. Are you a student?

Jack: **18** ....

Mrs Brown: It's very quiet here during the day. And the station's not far away.

Jack: **19** ....

Mrs Brown: Only in the road. I haven't got a garage.

Jack: **20** ....

Mrs Brown: All right. But before tomorrow.

A   What does the heating cost?

B   I can't decide about the room. Can I phone you later?

C   Can I use the kitchen and bathroom?

D   How near is the bus stop?

E   I like the big window – it's nice and sunny.

F   But is there anywhere to park my car?

G   Yes, I've come about the room.

H   A nurse, so I often have to work at night.

Remember, the questions are in the same order as the information in the article.

☐ when Chloë started playing the violin

☐ what Chloë says about her life

☐ how Chloë feels about her teacher

☐ information about Chloë's sister

☐ her dad's job

Do this exercise before you answer questions 21–27. The text tells us lots of things about Chloë and her life. Here are 10 things that are in the text. Read the text, then put the 10 things in the list below into the same order as they are in the text. Put a number in the boxes next to each line. The first one has been done for you.

☐ a film Chloë was in

☐ her mum's job

1 where Chloë was born

☐ someone who teaches Chloë

☐ how old Chloë was when she played her first concerts

Now you know where the information is in the text, and what comes first and what comes next. Questions 21–27 are in the same order as the information in the text. So, the example will always be about something at the very beginning and question 27 will always be about something at the end of the text.

Read questions 21–27 and <u>underline</u> the part of the article where you find the information to answer the questions.

Now answer questions 21–27.

PART 4

QUESTIONS 21–27

Read the article about a young girl who plays the violin.
Are sentences 21–27 'Right' (A) or 'Wrong' (B)?
If there is not enough information to answer 'Right' (A) or 'Wrong' (B), choose 'Doesn't say' (C).
For questions 21–27, mark A, B or C on your answer sheet.

Chloë Hanslip

Chloë was born in England. Her father works with computers and her mother teaches dance. Chloë began playing the violin when she was two. Her parents bought her a special violin which was small enough for her to use, and, even at this age, she could play without help. Her sister Virginia, who was nineteen at the time, played the piano and, after Chloë heard her play something, she tried to play it on her violin. From the age of four, she played at a number of concerts in Britain and America and in 1999 she was a child violinist in the Hollywood film *Onegin*.

Many teachers offered to give Chloë lessons but when she was seven she met Professor Zakhar Bron. She was certain from the beginning that he was the right teacher for her. His work takes him around the world and each year Chloë flies thousands of kilometres to get to his classes.

Chloë was only fourteen when she made her first CD, but she says she is just like any other teenager. 'I have lots of friends and I love pop music. Getting better on the violin is important, but I also make sure I have time for other things.'

Example:

0 Chloë's mother gives dance classes.

   A Right   **B** Wrong   **C** Doesn't say   *Answer:* | 0 | A B C |

----

21 Chloë's first violin was the same size as other violins.

   A Right   **B** Wrong   **C** Doesn't say

22 To start with, Chloë practised the same music as her sister.

   A Right   **B** Wrong   **C** Doesn't say

23 Chloë prefers playing concerts in America to playing in Britain.

   A Right   **B** Wrong   **C** Doesn't say

24 When Chloë first met Zakhar Bron, she knew she wanted to study with him.

   A Right   **B** Wrong   **C** Doesn't say

25 Chloë travels to other countries for her lessons with Zakhar Bron.

   A Right   **B** Wrong   **C** Doesn't say

26 Chloë thinks she has a different life from other people her age.

   A Right   **B** Wrong   **C** Doesn't say

27 Chloë plays pop music on the violin for her friends.

   A Right   **B** Wrong   **C** Doesn't say

TIP

Ask some simple questions about the text to help you understand it.

Read the article and try to answer these questions.

1 What is the article about? Is it about a person, an animal or a place?

2 Is the title of the article singular or plural?

3 What tense are most of the verbs in this text?

4 Does the text tell a story or does it give information?

5 Can you see any conjunctions (these are words like: 'and', 'because', 'but', 'if', 'so', 'or', 'while') in the text? Put a circle around the conjunctions in the text.

Now look at the verbs in these phrases from the text.

'badgers are'   'have … seen'
'are lots of '   'word for badger was'
'have been'   'are very old'   'have … found'
'badgers eat'   'they live'   'can'

Decide what tense they are in and put them in the right box in the table below.

present perfect	past	present

Now answer questions 28–35. The points below may help you.

Question 28

The word needs to go with the plural noun 'animals'.

Question 29

This part of a verb comes after the modal 'can'.

Question 30

This is about something happening over a long time ('centuries'), not a date in the past.

Question 31

This is about a single point in time in the past, '250,000 years ago'.

Question 32

This part of the verb comes after 'have' to make the present perfect tense.

Question 33

This is talking about a general fact.

Question 34

Read the whole sentence. The word must go with the phrase 'but in others'.

Question 35

This is in the present tense and must go with 'badgers'.

PART 5

Read the article about badgers.
Choose the best word (A, B or C) for each space.
For questions 28–35, mark A, B or C on your answer sheet.

Badgers

Not many people have **(0)** .... seen a badger. **(28)** ....
black and white animals can sometimes **(29)** .... the size of a
large dog. They live in underground holes in woods and forests in Europe
and many of their homes have been there **(30)** .... centuries.
Scientists have even found bones of badgers **(31)** 250,000
years ago. The old English word for a badger was 'brock' and a few
English villages, for example Brockenhurst and Brockley, have
(32) .... that name.

(33) .... are lots of children's books about badgers. In **(34)** .... stories badgers are very
old and clever, but in others they're not nice at all. Certainly, badgers are not very friendly and only
(35) .... out at night. They live on insects and small animals, but also eat young plants and eggs.

Example:

| 0 | **A** ever | **B** still | **C** soon | ***Answer:*** | 0 | A | B | C |

---

28   **A**   That   **B**   This   **C**   These

29   **A**   being   **B**   be   **C**   been

30   **A**   for   **B**   since   **C**   during

31   **A**   after   **B**   from   **C**   at

32   **A**   keeping   **B**   keep   **C**   kept

33   **A**   Here   **B**   There   **C**   They

34   **A**   some   **B**   any   **C**   every

35   **A**   came   **B**   come   **C**   comes

TIP

Count how many letters are needed for each word – this can help you with spelling.

Read each of the sentences, 0 and 36–40.

1 How many letters are there in each of the six words about places in a town?

2 Will any of the words you write need an extra 's' on the end of the word because they are plural?

Now look at the example.

Here are all six letters you need to spell the word, but there are two extra letters you must not use.

ACKMRETE

As you write the correct answer, cross out the letters you use.

For the example, the two extra letters are C and E.

Now answer questions 36–40 in the same way.

Question 36

A I B Y L R R E I

Question 37

M Z S M U S E U

Question 38

N S R E T U E T S A R A

Question 39

G E O L C D S L E

Question 40

E T H S A R T A E

PART 6

QUESTIONS 36–40

Read the descriptions of some places in a town.
What is the word for each one?
The first letter is already there. There is one space for each other letter in the word.
For questions 36–40, write the words on your answer sheet.

Example:

0   You can buy all your vegetables here.   m _ _ _ _ _

                                                                                        Answer:

0	market

---

36   You can read books here and take them home too,   l _ _ _ _ _ _
if you have a special card.

37   In this building, you can look at interesting old things.   m _ _ _ _ _

38   If you don't want to eat at home, you can buy a   r _ _ _ _ _ _ _ _
meal here.

39   Students are taught in classrooms here.   c _ _ _ _ _ _

40   You buy a ticket to watch a play here.   t _ _ _ _ _ _

Think about what kind of word is needed in each space.

Before you read the text, practise finding verbs, prepositions, pronouns, conjunctions and articles.

Read this short text and put a box around the verbs, a straight line under the prepositions, a wavy line under the pronouns, a circle around the conjunctions, and a triangle around the articles.

> Polly walked into a shoe shop and looked at the shoes. She really liked the red ones but they were too small. She asked the shop assistant to get a bigger pair. The shop assistant climbed up to the top shelf and got the bigger size. He gave them to Polly and she tried them on. They were beautiful and just right.

Now, read Barbara's letter to her friend Kate and think about what kind of word will go in each space. Here are some points to help you.

Example

This verb form comes after 'will' to talk about the future.

Question 41

This is a preposition that comes before a date.

Question 42

This is the 'going to' future and it needs to fit with 'Mum and Dad'.

Question 43

This is a preposition that goes with 'take'.

Question 44

This is a pronoun that refers back to 'Hannah'.

Question 45

This is a conjunction that means 'plus'.

Question 46

This is a modal verb that goes with 'to' plus another verb.

Question 47

This is a verb that means something you do with 'food'.

Question 48

This is a conjunction you use to talk about things that 'may' happen.

Question 49

This is a preposition that tells you where something happens.

Question 50

This is a verb that means 'to wish something for the future'.

Now answer questions 41–50.

PART 7

QUESTIONS 41–50

Complete the letter.
Write ONE word for each space.
For questions 41–50, write the words on your answer sheet.

Example:

0	be

Dear Kate,

It will **(0)** .... my 14th birthday **(41)** .... March 8. Mum and Dad **(42)** .... going to take me to the beach. We'll go by car, so I can take four friends **(43)** .... me.

Would you like to come? Hannah has said **(44)** .... will come. I am asking David, Maria **(45)** .... you. Mum will take all the food, so you don't **(46)** .... to bring anything to **(47)** ....

(48) .... the weather is good, we may swim **(49)** .... the sea so remember to bring your swimming things.

I really **(50)** .... you can come.

Love,
Barbara

Underline all the important information that you need to fill out the form or notes. Think about what you need to write for your answers: a word or a number.

First, look at David's notes about a shopping trip.

Underline the important words in his notes at the bottom of the page.

Now look at the advertisement and the email and underline this information:

1 all the shop names
2 all the cities
3 all the dates
4 all the places where they can meet
5 all the a.m. times
6 all the prices

Now that you have all the possible answers, you need to decide which one is correct. Let's look at question 51 together. There are three cities in the advertisement because Cresswell's has shops in all three cities. But if you look at Robert's email you can see that Robert and David are going to go to London. So 'London' is the answer to question 51.

Now answer questions 52–55.

PART 8

QUESTIONS 51–55

Read the advertisement and the email.
Fill in the information in David's notes.
For questions 51–55, write the information on your answer sheet.

CRESSWELL'S DEPARTMENT STORE

London, Manchester, Edinburgh

SALE

5 – 10 January

Computers £550 – were £850!

To: David

From: Robert

I know you wanted to buy a computer so let's go to Cresswell's on the first day of the sale. Computers are £300 cheaper at the moment. There's a train to London at 7.10 a.m. Wait for me at the bus stop at 6.30 a.m. and we'll walk to the station together.

David's Notes – Shopping Trip

Name of shop:		Cresswell's
In which city:	**51**	
Date of trip:	**52**	
Where to meet Robert:	**53**	
Train leaves at:	**54**	a.m.
Cost of computer:	**55**	£

TIP

Make some notes before you write your answer. Always check your answer before you copy it onto the answer sheet.

Some Part 9 tasks do not have a message or note for you to read, they just have instructions, like the task on page 57.

Answer these questions.

1 What did you leave at your friend's house?

2 Why is this thing important to you?

3 Where in your friend's house did you leave it?

When you have an answer to each of these questions, you are ready to write your note to your friend.

Use the question paper to first make some notes and write your answer.

You then need to check your answer. Look at the grammar and spelling and make sure everything is correct before you copy your answer onto the answer sheet.

Read Marie's note below.

Dear Anna,

I have left at your housee my coat. It is very important because was present from my mother. I thing I left the coat in your hall.

Love, Marie

Marie gives all the information the task asks for: what she left, why it is important and where in the house it is. Marie got full marks for this note.

There are some mistakes in Marie's note. Some of the words are in the wrong order, there are two words missing and there are two spelling mistakes. Can you find them?

Rewrite Marie's note so there are no mistakes.

PART 9

QUESTION 56

Last night you were at a friend's house. You think you left something important there.
Write a note to your friend.

Say:

- **what** you have left

- **why** it is important

- **where** in the house you think it is.

Write 25–35 words.

Write the note on your answer sheet.

Listening ● PART 1

TIP

Read each question. Think about the tense (e.g. present, past) the question is in.

Look at the five questions and decide which tense most of the conversations will be in (past, present or future). How do you know this? Fill in the table. The first one has been done for you.

question	tense + how you know
1	*Present tense. The word 'doesn't' is in the present tense.*
2	
3	
4	
5	

Look at questions 2 and 3 and answer these questions.

1 What are the names of the subjects in question 2?
2 What are the three things the woman is doing in each picture in question 3?
3 What other words, like 'next' or 'first', tell us what order things happen in?

Thinking about the tense and the order of the information you hear can help you find the correct answer.

Now listen to the recording and answer questions 1–5.

PART 1

QUESTIONS 1–5

You will hear five short conversations.
You will hear each conversation twice.
There is one question for each conversation.
For questions 1–5, put a tick (✓) under the right answer.

Example:

0 How many people were at the meeting?

3	**13**	**30**
A ☐	B ☐	C ✓

1 What doesn't the girl like about her photo?

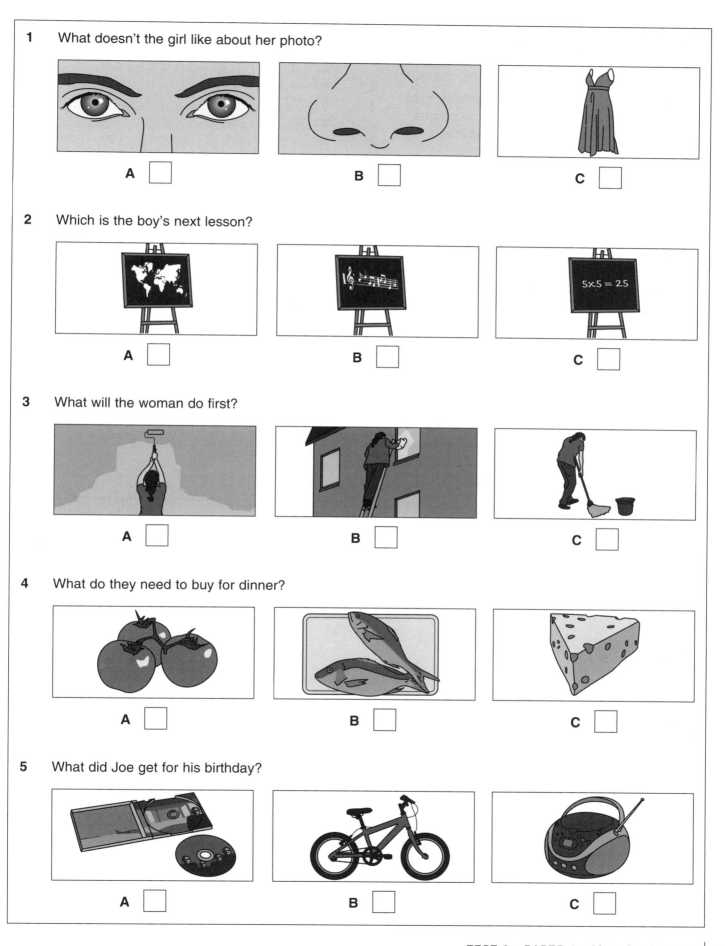

A ☐   B ☐   C ☐

2 Which is the boy's next lesson?

A ☐   B ☐   C ☐

3 What will the woman do first?

A ☐   B ☐   C ☐

4 What do they need to buy for dinner?

A ☐   B ☐   C ☐

5 What did Joe get for his birthday?

A ☐   B ☐   C ☐

TIP

Look at the task and think about the kind of conversation you will hear. Are the people talking about what they prefer, deciding something, choosing or explaining?

Look at everything written on the question paper. Answer these questions.

1 Who is talking?

2 What are they talking about?

3 What are the headings for the two lists, 6–10 and A–H?

4 Are the speakers choosing where to put each picture or explaining what each picture looks like?

In the table opposite there is a list of some of the things Gemma and Harry are doing in their conversation, like agreeing and disagreeing (not agreeing). Listen to the recording, stopping and starting when you want to. Try to fill in the table with the expressions you hear the people use. The first one has been done for you.

what the speakers are doing	expressions they use
agreeing	Good idea! OK. You're right. Great!
disagreeing	
talking about things they like	
talking about things they don't like	
asking for an idea	
giving an idea / making a suggestion	

Now listen to the recording and answer questions 6–10.

PART 2

QUESTIONS 6–10

Listen to Gemma and her husband, Harry, talking about pictures for their new house.
Which picture will they put in each room?
For questions 6–10, write a letter A–H next to each room.
You will hear the conversation twice.

Example:

0   living room | B |

Rooms

6   bathroom   [ ]

7   bedroom   [ ]

8   kitchen   [ ]

9   hall   [ ]

10 dining room   [ ]

Pictures

A   beach

B   cathedral

C   Gemma's parents

D   Harry's village

E   horses

F   mountains

G   racing cars

H   river

TIP

Think about what information you need to listen for.

Look at the instructions, the example and the five questions, 11–15.

Answer these questions.

1 What is Grace telling a friend about?

2 What is the name of the place Grace stayed at?

3 What do you think the friend asks Grace about before the answer to question 11?

4 What do you think the friend asks Grace about before the answer to question 12?

5 What do you think the friend asks Grace about before the answer to question 13?

6 In question 14, do you think Grace was happy with the food?

7 In question 15, do you think Grace was happy about the hotel in general?

Now listen to the recording, stopping and starting when you need to, and write down all the questions the friend asks Grace.

The friend's questions help you know when you have to listen carefully to find the right answers.

Now listen to the recording and answer questions 11–15.

PART 3

QUESTIONS 11–15

Listen to Grace telling a friend about a hotel.
For questions 11–15, tick (✓) A, B or C.
You will hear the conversation twice.

Example:

0	The name of the hotel is	**A**	Rosebank Hotel.	✓
		B	Rosewood Hotel.	
		C	Rosemount Hotel.	

11	The hotel is	**A**	in a town.	
		B	on a mountain.	
		C	near the sea.	
12	At the hotel, Grace could	**A**	play golf.	
		B	play tennis.	
		C	use the swimming pool.	
13	In Grace's room, there was	**A**	a fridge.	
		B	a video player.	
		C	a coffee machine.	
14	In the restaurant, Grace had	**A**	too few vegetables.	
		B	a lot of fried food.	
		C	chips with every meal.	
15	Grace says the hotel was	**A**	cheap.	
		B	boring.	
		C	noisy.	

TIP

Check your answers when you listen for the second time and when you copy your answers onto the answer sheet.

For questions 16–20 you have to write down information about a holiday English course. Look at the notes and decide what kind of information to listen for. Are you listening for numbers, times, dates, prices, ages, spellings of names or a word? Note the kind of information below.

Question 16 ....
Question 17 ....
Question 18 ....
Question 19 ....
Question 20 ....

Remember you will hear the conversation twice so do not worry if you are not sure about an answer the first time. When you listen the second time, you can also check that all your answers are correct.

Now listen to the recording and answer questions 16–20.

At the end of the test, you have to copy all your answers onto an answer sheet. This is when some candidates make mistakes. You need to check that you write each answer in the right place and that your handwriting is easy to read.

Here are the answers given by one candidate. What do you think about these answers? Will the candidate get a mark for each answer?

Part 4		Do not write here
16	thirteen years old or more	1 16 0
17	11	1 17 0
18	family	1 18 0
19	£ 619	1 19 0
20	Farlty	1 20 0

PART 4

QUESTIONS 16–20

You will hear a conversation about a holiday English course.
Listen and complete questions 16–20.
You will hear the conversation twice.

HOLIDAY ENGLISH COURSE

Place:		Oxford
Students must be:	**16**	.... years old or more
Starting date:	**17**	.... July.
Students stay with:	**18**	English ....
Price of course:	**19**	£
College in:	**20**	.... Street

Don't write more than you need to.

Before you listen, look at the instructions and notes about an air museum.

Answer these questions.

1 What kind of word must you listen for in question 21?
2 What information do you need to write down in question 22?
3 What will you write in question 23?
4 What will you need to write in question 24?
5 What will you write in question 25?

Now listen to the recording and answer questions 21–25.

When you have finished and checked the answers, look at one candidate's answers, opposite. What is the problem with these answers?

Part 5		Do not write here
21	The village of Cherford	1 21 0
22	Take the 51 bus from Cherford station	1 22 0
23	7.15pm and in winter closes at 4pm	1 23 0
24	For adults £6, for children/students £4.50, for families £18	1 24 0
25	Sundays –you should book seven days before	1 25 0

If you only need to write one or two words or a day or a number to answer the question, don't write more.

Part 5

QUESTIONS 21–25

You will hear some information about an air museum.
Listen and complete questions 21–25.
You will hear the information twice.

AIR MUSEUM

Museum has:	140 planes
Museum is near village of:	**21**
From village, get bus number:	**22**
Summer opening times:	**23** 10 a.m. to .... p.m.
Price of family ticket:	**24** £
Day for plane trips:	**25**

You now have 8 minutes to write your answers on the answer sheet.

The Speaking test lasts 8 to 10 minutes. You will take the test with another candidate. There are two examiners, but only one of them will talk to you. The examiner will ask you questions and ask you to talk to the other candidate.

Part 1 (5–6 minutes)

The examiner will ask you and your partner some questions. These questions will be about your daily life, past experience and future plans. For example, you may have to speak about your school, job, hobbies or home town.

Part 2 (3–4 minutes)

You and your partner will speak to each other. You will ask and answer questions. The examiner will give you a booklet with some information in it. The examiner will give your partner a booklet with some words in it. Your partner will use the words in the booklet to ask you questions about the information you have. Then you will change roles.

Speaking ● PART 1

TIP

Listen carefully to the examiner's questions.

In the first part of the test the examiner may ask you questions about your school, job, hobbies and family, and your likes and dislikes.

You can practise for this part of the test but be careful.

Do **not** learn the answers to lots of different questions because the examiner may not ask you the questions you have practised.

For example:

You practise the question and answer like this:

Question:

Where do you come from?

Answer:

I come from Spain.

But in the test the examiner asks you:

Where do you live?

The answer you practised, 'I come from Spain' is the wrong answer for that question.

You need to listen very carefully to the examiner and answer the questions he or she asks. Don't try to give the answers you have practised.

In the second part of the test you will need to find some information to answer your partner's questions.

Look at the information (2A) on page 132 about some football lessons.

Below are the five questions your partner asks you about the football lessons.

Read each question. Then look at the information in 2A and underline the words that answer these questions.

1   Where are the football lessons?

2   What days are the football lessons on?

3   Who are the football lessons for?

4   How much do the lessons cost?

5   What time are the lessons?

In the test, do not just read out the information in the task to answer your partner's questions. Put the information into full sentences when you answer.

For example:

Question: *Where are the football lessons?*

Answer: *The lessons are at the sports centre in North Road.*

Question: *What days are the football lessons on?*

Answer: *The lessons are every Tuesday and Friday.*

Now try to answer questions 3–5 with full sentences.

Now, if possible, practise giving full answers to the questions with another student. Use the task (2C and 2D) about a running race on pages 134 and 136.

TEST 3

Reading ● PART 1

TIP

Read each notice carefully. Look for words and phrases that have similar meanings.

When you read the sentences and notices, be careful to look for words and phrases that have similar meanings. Do not just look for words and phrases that are the same in the sentences and notices.

Read sentence 1.

1 What words in sentence 1 are also in the notices?

2 What words or phrases in sentence 1 have similar meanings to words and phrases in the notices?

Now read sentence 2.

3 What words in sentence 2 are also in the notices?

4 What words or phrases in sentence 2 have similar meanings to words and phrases in the notices?

You will see that just looking for the same word in the sentence and the notice will not find the right answer.

You need to look for words and phrases in the sentences and notices that have a similar meaning.

Now answer questions 1–5.

PART 1

QUESTIONS 1–5

Which notice (A–H) says this (1–5)?
For questions 1–5, mark the correct letter A–H on your answer sheet.

Example:

0   Get your ticket during your journey.

Answer:

0	A	B	C	D	E	F	G	H
	☐	☐	☐	☐	☐	☐	☐	▬

---

1   You cannot travel by railway until tomorrow.

A
> MUSEUM OF TRAVEL AND
> TRANSPORT
> *Entrance free for children*

B
> Please show your ticket at the
> museum entrance

2   Children and parents travel for less with this.

C
> GET CHEAPER TICKETS
> WITH A FAMILY RAILCARD

D
> NO TRAINS TODAY BECAUSE
> OF VERY HIGH WINDS

3   You must pay before you travel on this.

E
> TRAIN TICKETS WILL COST
> MORE FROM 1ST JANUARY

F
> 8.30 LONDON TRAIN
> DELAYED BECAUSE OF FOG

4   Only adults pay to go in here.

G
> DO NOT GET ON THE
> TRAIN WITHOUT A TICKET

5   This is late because of bad weather.

H
> TICKET OFFICE CLOSED
> BUY YOUR TICKET ON
> THE TRAIN

TIP

Think about the meaning of each word in the A, B and C options and how you would use the word in a sentence.

Part 2 tests vocabulary.

When you learn a new word in English, it is a good idea to put it in an example sentence. Then you can see how the word is used. A good English learners' dictionary will help you do this.

Answer questions 6–10 and fill in the gaps opposite at the same time. There are two more example sentences for each question, 6–10. Each of the three words from the A, B or C options will fit into one of the three sentences. Decide which word goes in each sentence.

Question 6

Indira has to take the customers to their table and .... them to sit down.

When the customers ...., Indira has to take them to a table.

Question 7

The customers sometimes .... Indira for a special dish.

Indira doesn't .... much English but she likes to practise with the customers.

Question 8

Indira always has to .... the bill to see it is correct.

Once, a customer asked Indira if she could .... pounds into dollars.

Question 9

Indira doesn't .... very much money on food as she gets free lunches.

Indira doesn't need to .... food when she's working, because she gets a free lunch.

Question 10

If Indira .... to go to university, she will stop working as a waitress.

Indira .... studying and wants to go to university in the future.

PART 2

QUESTIONS 6–10

Read the sentences about working as a waitress.
Choose the best word (A, B or C) for each space.
For questions 6–10 mark A, B or C on your answer sheet.

Example:

0   Indira is a waitress and works in a fast-food ....

    A   shop   **B**   restaurant   **C**   school

Answer:

0	A	B	C

----

6   Indira has to .... the customers and take them to a table.

    A   welcome   **B**   arrive   **C**   invite

7   The customers .... what they want to eat and Indira writes it down in a notebook.

    A   speak   **B**   ask   **C**   choose

8   Indira can .... any extra money which customers leave for her on the table.

    A   change   **B**   keep   **C**   check

9   If Indira has lunch at the restaurant, she doesn't have to .... for her food.

    A   buy   **B**   spend   **C**   pay

10   In a few years, Indira .... to study Food Science at university.

    A   hopes   **B**   likes   **C**   decides

TIP

Look at the A, B, C options. For each option, imagine what the first speaker said.

For each of these five conversations there are two people speaking to each other. On the left of the page is the first speaker. On the right of the page there are three different replies from the second speaker (A, B and C).

Look at question 11. Let's imagine what the first speaker says for all the options.

Now look at the table below. Match the first speaker's questions with the second speaker's replies. Draw a line to show which question goes with which answer. (The first one has been done for you.)

First speaker	Second speaker
Do you like this shirt?	They're both great.
Which shirt do you prefer?	Not so much.
What do you think about this shirt?	It's too big.

Now do the same with these sentences for question 12. Match the first speaker's sentences with the second speaker's replies.

First speaker	Second speaker
David gave his guitar to his brother.	What's the matter with him?
David isn't very well.	How long does he take?
David cycles to college every day.	Why did he do it?

Now do questions 13–15 and choose the best answer, A, B or C, for each one.

As you answer the questions, think about what the first speaker could say for each of the second speaker's replies. This will help you decide which is the correct answer.

PART 3

QUESTIONS 11–15

Complete the five conversations.
For questions 11–15, mark A, B or C on your answer sheet.

Example:
0

Where do you come from?

A New York.

B School.

C Home.

Answer:

0	A	B	C
	▬	▭	▭

---

11 Which shirt do you prefer?

A They're both great.

B Not so much.

C It's too big.

12 David isn't very well.

A What's the matter with him?

B How long does he take?

C Why did he do it?

13 How do you know my sister?

A We'll meet outside the cinema.

B We're in the same class.

C She's got blue eyes.

14 I hope Andrew will get here soon.

A I hope he hasn't.

B He usually gets it.

C I'm sure he will.

15 Who phoned me?

A It's Anne speaking.

B Sorry, I forgot to ask.

C I don't know your name.

TIP

After you put a sentence in a space, check that it fits with the sentence that comes before and after it.

Two friends, Mike and Steve, are talking about a camping trip.

Look at the example. Why is D the right answer here? Look at what Steve says before and after the example. To get the right answer, you have to look at the sentences that come both before and after the space.

Now look at questions 16–20 and think about the extra questions below.

Question 16

What kind of sentence, a question or a statement, must come before Steve saying, 'Not this year'?

Question 17

What is Mike asking about if Steve says, 'About a month' in his answer?

Question 18

After the gap, Steve says, 'I have an extra one you can use.' What does 'one' mean here?

Question 19

What do you say when someone does something nice for you?

Question 20

Before the space, Steve asks about Mike's past experience. What tense do you think Mike's answer will be in?

Now answer questions 16–20. When you have finished, check your answers by reading the whole conversation.

PART 3

QUESTIONS 16–20

Complete the conversation between two friends about a camping trip.
What does Mike say to Steve?
For questions 16–20, mark the correct letter A–H on your answer sheet.

Example:

Steve: Hi, Mike. What are you doing for your summer holiday?

Mike: **0** ....   ***Answer:***

Steve: I'm going camping with some friends.

Mike: **16** ....

Steve: Not this year. We're going to the forest.

Mike: **17** ....

Steve: About a month, I think. Would you like to come with us?

Mike: **18** ....

Steve: That doesn't matter, I have an extra one you can use.

Mike: **19** ....

Steve: Have you ever been camping before?

Mike: **20** ....

Steve: Well, I'm sure we'll have a great time.

A   Only once, when I was very young.

B   It's a very long way to the forest.

C   Thanks very much, Steve.

D   I'm not sure yet. What about you?

E   I'd love to, but I haven't got a tent.

F   How long are you going to stay?

G   I'm afraid I can't. I'm busy.

H   Really? Are you going to the beach?

Always read the instructions and look at the title and picture first. This gives you a lot of information about what you are going to read.

1   What do you know about Rob from the title and picture?

Now look at questions 21–27 and the example. You can learn about the article by reading the questions.

In the example we learn that Rob is not American.

What information can you learn or guess about the text from the other questions? Match the questions with the pieces of information.

Question 21
Question 22
Question 23
Question 24
Question 25
Question 26
Question 27

Rob's father was at the play.

The text talks about Shakespeare's plays.

Rob has acted again since the school play.

Rob played an old man in the play.

There are guests at his birthday.

Rob acted in a school play.

Rob has a birthday in the text.

So the questions can help us understand what we are going to read in the text. Now read the text and answer questions 21–27.

PART 4

QUESTIONS 21–27

Read the article about Rob Stone.
Are sentences 21–27 'Right' (A) or 'Wrong' (B)?
If there is not enough information to answer 'Right' (A) or 'Wrong' (B), choose 'Doesn't say' (C).
For questions 21–27, mark A, B or C on your answer sheet.

Rob Stone and the school play

Last week, Rob Stone, the famous British actor and star of many Hollywood films, had a party for his 53rd birthday. Rob invited a lot of other actors to his beautiful home for his party. After dinner, he stood up and spoke to everyone there. He told them about something that happened when he was at school 40 years ago. As a schoolboy, Rob loved the theatre and he was very happy when he had his first part in a play. It was a very sad play by Shakespeare, the sixteenth-century English writer.

Rob played the part of an old man who had to die on stage. He practised and practised to become good at the part. He had to lie on a bed, say a few sad words of goodbye to his sons and then shout in pain and die.

Like all the other parents, Mr and Mrs Stone came to watch their son in the play. Rob told his guests, 'I shall never forget that evening. It was terrible. As I died, I could hear my father laughing! I still remember now how bad I felt and I have not asked my father to one of my plays since.'

Example:

0 Rob Stone comes from America.

   A Right   **B** Wrong   **C** Doesn't say   *Answer:* | 0 | A ▢ B ▬ C ▢ |

- -

21 Rob Stone went to a restaurant for his birthday.

   A Right   **B** Wrong   **C** Doesn't say

22 Rob talked to a few of his guests about his time at school.

   A Right   **B** Wrong   **C** Doesn't say

23 Rob preferred Shakespeare's plays to those of any other writer.

   A Right   **B** Wrong   **C** Doesn't say

24 Rob tried very hard to act well in the school play.

   A Right   **B** Wrong   **C** Doesn't say

25 The old man that Rob played died at the end of the play.

   A Right   **B** Wrong   **C** Doesn't say

26 Rob's father made his son unhappy at the play.

   A Right   **B** Wrong   **C** Doesn't say

27 Rob never invited his father to watch him act again.

   A Right   **B** Wrong   **C** Doesn't say

TIP

Try each word from the A, B and C options in the gap before you choose your answers. Why are two of them wrong?

Look at the example and say the sentence to yourself three times:

1 People love dolphins because **they** are beautiful to watch and friendly.

2 People love dolphins because **we** are beautiful to watch and friendly.

3 People love dolphins because **you** are beautiful to watch and friendly.

All three words are pronouns but 'we' and 'you' do not fit with 'dolphins' because 'we' means the 'writer and another person', and 'you' means the 'reader'. Only 'they' can fit with 'dolphins'. Now look at options A, B and C for each question, 28–35, in the same way.

Here is a list of reasons why one answer is correct and the other two are wrong. Match the reasons with questions 28–35. The first one has been done for you.

Question 28 — This preposition goes with the word 'mistake'.

Question 29 — This word means dolphins are similar to other sea animals.

Question 30 — 'Dolphins' is plural and the text is in the present tense.

Question 31 — This pronoun is often used as the subject of a sentence giving general information.

Question 32 — This word makes a comparative adjective stronger.

Question 33 — This word shows the writer is surprised by some people's ideas about dolphins.

Question 34 — Dolphins are one part of a bigger group of animals.

Question 35 — This verb has to end in *-ing* because it follows the preposition 'of'.

Now do questions 28–35.

PART 5

Read the article about dolphins.
Choose the best word (A, B or C) for each space.
For questions 28–35, mark A, B or C on your answer sheet.

DOLPHINS

People love dolphins because **(0)** .... are beautiful to watch and friendly.
Dolphins are also **(28)** .... of the cleverest animals and are just as clever
as dogs. **(29)** .... is possible to teach them in the same way we teach
monkeys and dogs. Some people **(30)** .... believe that dolphins have a
special way of **(31)** .... to each other.

(32) .... many other sea animals and fish, dolphins are in danger. Many dolphins are caught
(33) .... mistake in fishing nets, but a **(34)** .... greater problem is that thousands of
dolphins **(35)** .... dying because the sea is no longer clean enough.

Example:

0	**A** they	**B** we	**C** you

Answer:

0	A	B	C
	▄▄	▢	▢

----

28   **A**   another   **B**   one   **C**   all

29   **A**   There   **B**   It   **C**   This

30   **A**   quite   **B**   yet   **C**   even

31   **A**   talking   **B**   talk   **C**   talked

32   **A**   As   **B**   For   **C**   Like

33   **A**   with   **B**   by   **C**   from

34   **A**   more   **B**   much   **C**   most

35   **A**   were   **B**   is   **C**   are

Underline the important words in each
sentence, 36–40.

Part 6 tests your vocabulary and your spelling.
Read the instructions. This task is about words
about clothes so start thinking about all the words
about clothes that you know.

Here are some exercises to help you think of some
words. Look at the example. The important word
to underline here is 'head'. This helps find the
answer, 'hat'.

The first table has a list of other parts of the body.
Think of the name for the clothes we wear on that
part of the body. Fill in the table.

part of the body	clothes
head	hat
hands	
neck	
chest, back and arms	
legs	
feet	

What special clothes do we wear when we are in
these different places?

place	clothes
at school	
on a beach	
at work	
on a motorbike	
at a sports centre	

Can you think of the clothes we wear at different
times of year?

time of year	clothes
winter	
spring	
summer	
autumn	

Now answer questions 36–40. Did filling in the
tables help you think of some of the answers?

PART 6

Read the descriptions of some words about clothes.
What is the word for each one?
The first letter is already there. There is one space for each other letter in the word.
For questions 36–40, write the words on your answer sheet.

Example:

0   This keeps your head warm.   h _ _

Answer: | 0 | hat |

----

36   Some boys and girls have to wear this at school.   u _ _ _ _ _ _

37   This is often on a shirt and you can put pens in it.   p _ _ _ _ _

38   People wear this in the winter when they go outside.   c _ _ _

39   This is the top part of a suit for men and women.   j _ _ _ _ _

40   You wear these on your feet, inside your shoes.   s _ _ _ _

TIP

Make sure the word you choose fits with the information before and after the space.

Here is a text with eight mistakes in it. The mistakes are <u>underlined</u>. Can you correct them? Think about the words that come before and after the mistake because the word you choose must fit with them.

I'm writing this postcard <u>at</u> you from Spain. We're staying in <u>an</u> great place and meeting <u>lot</u> of new people. Next to our room <u>here</u> is a really nice family, with two boys the same age as <u>mine</u>. One of <u>these</u> has a sailing boat so we often <u>going</u> sailing in <u>an</u> afternoon.

Now read Kenny's email to his friend Paul and think what word will go in each space.

Here are some points to help you.

Example

This preposition often goes with the verb 'to send'.

Question 41

'Excellent' begins with the vowel 'e'.

Question 42

'Words' is plural.

Question 43

This tells us more about the family.

Question 44

This refers back to the 'boys'.

Question 45

This is about a future plan.

Question 46

Paul can choose to get an email every day or not.

Question 47

This is a preposition.

Question 48

This verb is often used with 'swimming'.

Question 49

This is a preposition.

Question 50

This pronoun refers to Kenny, the writer.

Now answer questions 41–50.

PART 7

Complete the email from Kenny to his friend Paul.
Write ONE word for each space.
For questions 41–50, write the words on your answer sheet.

Example:

0	to

From:	Kenny
To:	Paul

Hi Paul,

I'm sending this email **(0)** .... you from France! I'm having
(41) .... excellent time here in Lyon and learning a
(42) .... of new words on my language course.

I'm staying with a great family. **(43)** .... are two teenage boys and
one of **(44)** .... has got a computer in his room. I **(45)** ....
send you an email every day **(46)** .... you like. They've also got a
pool **(47)** .... the garden and after college I often **(48)** ....
swimming.

How's everything **(49)** .... home? Write to **(50)** .... soon,

Kenny

Check the spelling of your answers. You need to copy them carefully.

First, look at the notice, email and Hannah's notes and try to answer questions 51–55.

Now look at this candidate's answer sheet and the answers they wrote.

How many questions did this candidate get right? If they got an answer wrong, why was it wrong?

Remember, all the spellings and numbers are correct on the question paper. Be careful not to make mistakes when you copy your answers onto the answer sheet. It is also a good idea to use capital letters so that your writing is easy to read.

Part 8		Do not write here
51	977866	1 51 0
52	Wensday	1 52 0
53	7 May	1 53 0
54	three	1 54 0
55	corpork	1 55 0

PART 8

Read the notice and email about a football team.
Fill in the information in Hannah's notes.
For questions 51–55, write the information on your answer sheet.

SOUTHSIDE
FOOTBALL TEAM

Weekly practice starts
Wednesday, 7 May.

11 – 14 years – Wednesday, 3p.m.
15 – 17 years – Friday, 4p.m.

Parents should wait for
children in the car park.

First match at City College
20 May. Call Sue Harris on
977886 for other dates.

From:	Hannah Jones
To:	Miss Harris

I am 13 and I want to join the football team. I am on holiday until 9 May so I will come on 14 May. My phone number is 886655.

HANNAH'S NOTES – FOOTBALL PRACTICE

Name of team: Southside

Phone no. for more information: **51**

My practice day: **52**

My start date: **53**

Time: **54** p.m.

Place to meet Dad: **55**

TIP

Make sure you write in full sentences and check your punctuation.

Look at the note from your friend Jo.

Answer these questions:

1 Do you go to the same school as Jo?

2 What kind of class will you both go to?

3 What has Jo lost?

Now <u>underline</u> the three questions in the note that Jo wants you to answer.

You must answer each of these questions in your note to Jo.

Remember, when you write your answer you need to use full sentences. Look at this note to Jo. Decide where the sentences should be. Put a capital letter at the beginning of each sentence and a full stop at the end. What other words should have capitals? Correct Jan's note to Jo.

dear jo
the class is on monday it is a very good class it is three hours long you don't have to bring anything.
love jan

How many of Jo's questions does Jan answer?

PART 9

QUESTION 56

Read this note from your friend Jo.

> I can't find the information about the new art class after school. What day is the class? How long is it? What do we have to bring with us?
>
> Thanks,
>
> Jo

Write a note to Jo and answer the questions.

Write 25–35 words.

Write the note on your answer sheet.

Listening ● PART 1

TIP

Don't worry if you miss the answer the first time. You will hear each conversation twice.

Look at questions 1–5 and answer these questions before you listen to the recording.

Question 1

What are the three times in the pictures? Say them out loud to yourself in different ways. For example, A is either 'five thirty' or 'half past five'.

Question 2

What are the three things in each picture?

Question 3

Where are the chairs in the pictures?

Question 4

What are the three clothes sizes? Say them out loud.

Question 5

What are the three types of ice cream?

Before you listen to the recording, look at questions 1–5 and think about what information you have to listen for.

For example, in question 1 you need to listen for the time the taxi will 'arrive' at the woman's house, not 'leave'.

In question 2, you will hear two people talking about giving all three things to George, but they will decide on *only one* of them.

In question 3, the two people will talk about all three places but decide to sit in *only one* of them.

In question 4, you will hear all three sizes but the woman will *only buy one*.

In question 5, you will hear all three words, 'coffee', 'chocolate' and 'banana', but *only one* is the ice cream the people in the conversation will eat.

Now listen to the recording, but only listen to each conversation once, not twice. After you have listened once only, listen to the conversations again, and check your answers while listening.

If you do more listening practice, you will be able to get most of these questions right just by listening once.

Remember, in the test you will hear each conversation twice, so you will be able to check your answers when you listen the second time.

PART 1

QUESTIONS 1–5

You will hear five short conversations.
You will hear each conversation twice.
There is one question for each conversation.
For questions 1–5, put a tick (✓) under the right answer.

Example:

0 How many people were at the meeting?

3	**13**	**30**
A ☐	B ☐	C ✓

1 What time will the taxi arrive at the woman's house?

A ☐

B ☐

C ☐

2 What will they give George?

A ☐

B ☐

C ☐

3 Where will they sit?

A ☐

B ☐

C ☐

4 What size does the woman buy?

38	**40**	**42**
A ☐	B ☐	C ☐

5 Which ice cream will they have?

A ☐

B ☐

C ☐

TIP

Think about other ways of saying the words given in the list A–H.

Before you listen, look at everything written on the question paper for this part.

Answer these questions.

1　Who is Laura talking to?
2　What is Laura talking about?
3　What are the headings for the two lists, 6–10 and A–H?
4　Which letter, A–H, can you not use as an answer?

Before you listen to the recording, look at the list of problems in the table opposite.

Can you think of another way to say the problem?

Look at the example for 'closed', then fill in the table.

Problems	Is there another way to say this?
A closed	shut, not open
B cold	
C dirty	
D expensive	
E full	
F hot	
G noisy	
H wet	

Now listen to the recording and answer questions 6–10.

Did it help you to think about other ways of saying the problems before you listened?

PART 2

QUESTIONS 6–10

Listen to Laura talking to a friend about places to go.
What is the problem with each place?
For questions 6–10, write a letter A–H next to each place.
You will hear the conversation twice.

Example:

0   cinema | F |

Places

6   restaurant | |

7   disco | |

8   swimming pool | |

9   theatre | |

10 sports field | |

Problems

A   closed

B   cold

C   dirty

D   expensive

E   full

F   hot

G   noisy

H   wet

Remember that in this part of the test you will need to listen for places, numbers, days of the week, prices, dates, times, etc.

Before you listen, look at the words in the box below.

They are the things you need to listen for to answer questions 11–15

Now look at the five questions, 11–15.

Match each question with a word from the second column. The example is done for you.

question	information you need to listen for
Example	clothes
11	dates
12	places
13	jobs
14	numbers
15	times

Now think of questions the girl and the man at the job information centre may ask.

	girl's question	man's question
Example	What kind of jobs are there?	What kind of job do you want?
Question 11		
Question 12		
Question 13		
Question 14		
Question 15		

Now listen to the recording and answer questions 11–15.

PART 3

QUESTIONS 11–15

Listen to a girl speaking to a man at a job information centre.
For questions 11–15, tick (✓) A, B or C.
You will hear the conversation twice.

Example:

0   The man has a job for a

    A   cleaner. ☐

    B   receptionist. ✓

    C   waitress. ☐

---

11   The job is in

    A   a hotel. ☐

    B   a sports centre. ☐

    C   an office. ☐

12   You cannot do the job if you are younger than

    A   18. ☐

    B   19. ☐

    C   20. ☐

13   The job will begin on the

    A   23rd. ☐

    B   24th. ☐

    C   26th. ☐

14   Most working days will begin at

    A   8.15 a.m. ☐

    B   8.30 a.m. ☐

    C   9.00 a.m. ☐

15   For work, the girl must wear

    A   a white shirt. ☐

    B   a blue skirt. ☐

    C   black trousers. ☐

For questions 16–20, you have to write down the answers a woman gives to a man's questions about a holiday.

Before you listen, look at the notes about a holiday in Ireland and think about what questions the man asks.

Now read what the man actually asks the woman about the hotel. These are the questions but they are in the wrong order. Put them into the order you think you will hear them on the recording. Put a number in each box.

How much does the holiday cost?	☐
How do you spell that?	☐
Can you give me some information about your short holidays in Ireland?	☐
Can I book two places for next weekend?	☐
What's the hotel like?	☐

Now listen to the recording to see if you got the questions in the right order.

Listen to the recording again and answer questions 16–20.

PART 4

QUESTIONS 16–20

You will hear a man asking for information about a holiday in Ireland.
Listen and complete questions 16–20.
You will hear the conversation twice.

HOLIDAY IN IRELAND

Leave on:		*Friday morning*
Number of nights:	**16**	
Name of hotel:	**17**	
Coach trip to visit:	**18**	a .... *factory*
Price this month:	**19**	£ .... *per person*
Date of holiday:	**20**	*17th* ....

Don't always think the first thing you hear is the correct answer, even if it is the right kind of information.

Before you listen, look at the information about a fire practice at a school. What kind of information are you listening for in each question?

Now listen to the recording, stopping and starting when you need to, and quickly write down all the pieces of information that might be answers; for example, all the times of the day.

You will see that for every question, except question 23, there are two times, things, places and activities. Some of the information is already in the notes, such as 'bags' and 'run', so that will help you.

In question 24 you need to be careful and listen to everything. If you write down the first place you hear (the car park), you will be wrong.

Now listen to the recording and answer questions 21–25.

PART 5

QUESTIONS 21–25

You will hear a head teacher giving students some information about a fire practice.
Listen and complete questions 21–25.
You will hear the information twice.

FIRE PRACTICE

Day:		*Monday*
Starting time:	**21**	.... *a.m.*
Don't take:	**22**	.... *or bags*
Go out of building through:	**23**	.... *door*
Outside, wait next to:	**24**	
Don't:	**25**	*run or* ....

You now have 8 minutes to write your answers on the answer sheet.

The Speaking test lasts 8 to 10 minutes. You will take the test with another candidate. There are two examiners, but only one of them will talk to you. The examiner will ask you questions and ask you to talk to the other candidate.

Part 1 (5–6 minutes)
The examiner will ask you and your partner some questions. These questions will be about your daily life, past experience and future plans. For example, you may have to speak about your school, job, hobbies or home town.

Part 2 (3–4 minutes)
You and your partner will speak to each other. You will ask and answer questions. The examiner will give you a booklet with some information in it. The examiner will give your partner a booklet with some words in it. Your partner will use the words in the booklet to ask you questions about the information you have. Then you will change roles.

Speaking ● PART 1

TIP

Look at the examiner when you speak to them.

In the first part of the test the examiner will be talking to you and asking you questions about your life – about things like your school, job, hobbies and family.

Remember, the examiner is friendly and wants you to do well in the test.

Don't be afraid of the examiner. If you don't hear or understand what the examiner says, ask them to say it again.

Here are some ways of asking the examiner to repeat or explain something:

Can you say that again, please?

I'm sorry. I don't understand …

Do you mean …?

Would you mind repeating that?

Make sure you know how to use these phrases but don't use them too often in the test. You should be listening carefully to the examiner.

TIP

Listen carefully to the examiner and your partner, and if you don't understand something, ask them to say it again.

In the second part of the test both you and your partner will have to do a task where you ask and answer questions.

When the examiner gives you the task, listen carefully to the examiner's instructions. If you don't understand something, ask the examiner to say it again. If you don't understand your partner when he or she asks or answers the questions, ask your partner to say it again.

Try to think of the different ways you can ask someone to say something again. Remember, we looked at some examples in the exercise for Speaking Part 1. Can you remember them?

Practise the task about a sailing school on pages 131 (3A) and 133 (3B) with a partner.

Every time they ask a question, pretend you do not understand and ask them to say it again. Remember to be polite!

Now change over, so the other person is asking the questions, and do the same thing, asking them to say it again, with the task about a job advertisement on pages 135 (3C) and 137 (3D).

TEST 4

Reading ● PART 1

TIP

Read each notice and decide what the topic of the notice is.

The notices in Part 1 are usually on one or two (sometimes three) different topics like travel or shopping.

Look at notices A–H and decide which notice goes in which topic group.

Fill in the table below by writing the letters A–H in the correct box.

topic	notice
travel	
shopping	
restaurants	

You can also group the notices in other ways. For example, fill in this table by answering these two questions.

	notice
Which notices have phone numbers?	
Which notices have times/dates?	

Now you know a lot about the notices and can answer questions 1–5.

PART 1

QUESTIONS 1–5

Which notice (A–H) says this (1–5)?
For questions 1–5, mark the correct letter A–H on your answer sheet.

Example:

0   You can't travel very early in the morning if you want to buy this ticket.

Answer:

0	A	B	C	D	E	F	G	H
	▭	▭	▭	▭	▭	▭	▬	▭

---

1   If you want to do something special for your child's birthday, call this number.

A
> **For times of afternoon coach trips, please ask hotel receptionist**

B
> **Telephone:**
> 2222 for motorway news and
> 2223 for airport information

2   This company can take you to catch your plane at any time.

C
> *Many children's toys and books half price*
> *This weekend only!*

D
> **Ask your waiter for our under-12s' menu**

3   If you need to buy something to wear, this may be the cheapest place to look.

E
> **HARRISONS DEPARTMENT STORE**
> NEW SEASON'S JACKETS —
> LOWEST PRICES IN TOWN

4   This restaurant always has special meals for children.

F
> **Star Restaurant** ★
> Children's Party Room
> Open at weekends
> Bookings ☎ 791053

G
> *For cheap day return tickets, you must travel after 10am*

5   If you need to know about the traffic, you can call this number.

H
> **JENNI'S AIRPORT TAXIS**
> (☎ 433587)
> 24 hours / 7 days a week

TIP

Read all the sentences together. Sometimes they tell a short story.

It is a good idea to read all the sentences together, before you start to answer. Then you will have a better idea about the topic of the sentences.

Read the sentences about a birthday present, but do not look at the words A–C. Now answer these questions.

1 Whose birthday was it?

2 What problem did Michael have?

3 What is one of Michael's sister's hobbies?

4 Why couldn't Michael get his sister a camera?

5 Which present was too expensive for Michael?

6 Who did Michael ask for help?

7 How was Michael feeling – happy or sad?

8 Did Michael's sister give him any ideas for a present?

Now answer questions 6–10.

Remember to check your answers by reading the sentences to yourself.

PART 2

Read the sentences about a birthday present.
Choose the best word (A, B or C) for each space.
For questions 6–10, mark A, B or C on your answer sheet.

Example:

0   Michael wanted to .... his sister a present for her
birthday.

    A   buy   **B**   sell   **C**   do

Answer:

---

6   Michael didn't .... what kind of present to get his sister.

    A   think   **B**   know   **C**   understand

7   His sister liked .... photographs but she already had a camera.

    A   making   **B**   putting   **C**   taking

8   He wanted to get her a TV but that meant spending too much ....

    A   money   **B**   price   **C**   cost

9   He asked a friend to help because the problem was making him ....

    A   afraid   **B**   unhappy   **C**   difficult

10   Michael's sister told him it didn't .... what present he gave her.

    A   prefer   **B**   mind   **C**   matter

TIP

Check your answers before you write them on the answer sheet.

When you are doing the KET exam, you can write on the question paper. You can put a circle round the answer, A, B or C. You can draw a line from what the first speaker says, to the answer A, B or C.

Look at the conversations in this test. Now look at the table below. For each conversation in questions 11–15, match 'Who is talking?' and 'What are they talking about?' from the table.

The example has been done for you.

Question	Who is talking?	What are they talking about?
Example	two people meeting for the first time	a visit from a family member
11	mother and son	saying goodbye
12	two friends	not understanding the teacher
13	two schoolfriends	when to have a meeting
14	two people meeting for the first time	the place they live
15	two work colleagues	being late for school

Now do questions 11–15 and choose the best answer, A, B or C, for each one.

Remember to check your answers. One way to do this is to say the conversations to yourself, silently.

If you want more practice, think of and write down your own short conversations.

For example:

A father talking to his daughter about her first day at a new school.

Father: Did you enjoy your first day at school, Helen?

Helen: It was OK but the maths class was difficult!

Here are some more ideas to help you.

1   A man in a shop talking to an assistant about the price of something.

2   Two friends talking about what they did last weekend.

3   One friend asking another about the homework they have to do.

When you are happy with your conversations, read them to yourself or, if possible, with another student in your class or with a friend.

PART 3

QUESTIONS 11–15

Complete the five conversations.
For questions 11–15, mark A, B or C on your answer sheet.

Example:
0

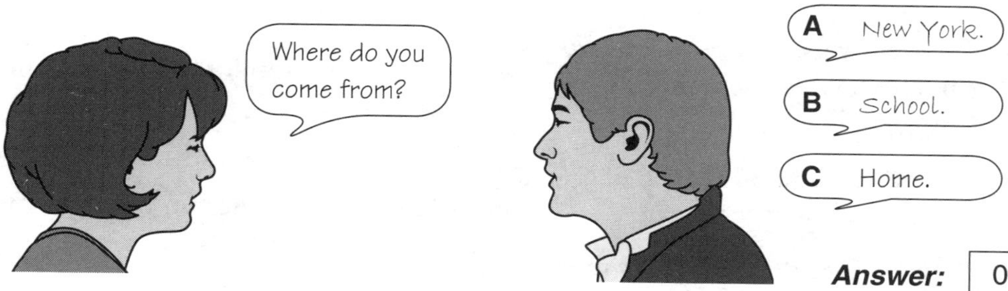
Where do you come from?
A New York.
B School.
C Home.

Answer:

0	A	B	C
	▬	▭	▭

---

11 Are you going to get up soon?

A In a minute.
B Not long.
C For ever.

12 My aunt is going to stay with me.

A How do you do?
B How long for?
C How was it?

13 Did you understand what she was saying?

A It's not enough.
B I'm sure she wasn't.
C Not really.

14 Nice to meet you, Suzanna.

A Yes, and you.
B Yes, I have.
C I think so.

15 Are you free this Tuesday?

A I can be, if it's important.
B Sorry I'm late.
C Not very often.

TIP

Remember that you cannot use any of the sentences A–H more than once.

When you first read this conversation between two friends, Raya and Joel, check which sentence, A–H, is the answer to the example.

Here, the answer is F so put a line through F like this: F̷.

This will help you to remember that you can't use that sentence again.

Read the left side of the page first and see how much you understand.

Answer these questions:

1 How much homework does Joel have?

2 Why is Joel going to his cousin's house?

3 Where do you think he is going to go on the bus?

4 What do you think the 'it' means in Joel's question?

5 Which subject does Joel find difficult?

Now look at the replies on the right of the page and answer questions 16–20.

When you think you have the right answer for a space, use a pencil to put a line through the letter.

PART 3

Complete the conversation about some homework.
What does Raya say to Joel?
For questions 16–20, mark the correct letter A–H on your answer sheet.

Example:

Joel: Hello, Raya. How are you?

Raya: **0** ....

Answer:

0	A	B	C	D	E	F	G	H
	▭	▭	▭	▭	▭	▬	▭	▭

Joel: I'm fine, but I've got lots of homework to do tonight.

Raya: **16** ....

Joel: Because my computer's not working. I'm going to my cousin's house to use hers.

Raya: **17** ....

Joel: It's a short journey on the bus.

Raya: **18** ....

Joel: Are you sure? Don't you need it this evening?

Raya: **19** ....

Joel: Have you? Even the maths? I can't understand any of it!

Raya: **20** ....

Joel: That's kind.

A   It's quite easy really. I'll help you.

B   The maths was easier than the other homework.

C   How far away is that?

D   Really? So why aren't you at home studying?

E   What's wrong with your computer?

F   Fine thanks, Joel. And you?

G   I've finished all my homework for tomorrow.

H   I live five minutes from here. Why don't you come and use my computer?

TIP

Always read the whole paragraph before you answer a question.

There are three paragraphs in this article about some beautiful old cups. Look at the questions, but before you answer them, decide which paragraph the answer will be in for each of the questions. Do this by reading the questions and the paragraphs as quickly as you can.

Paragraph 1   Questions ....
Paragraph 2   Questions ....
Paragraph 3   Questions ....

The article about cups and the questions have many pronouns.

Look at the list of pronouns opposite. Which ones are used in the article?

I   he   she   they   them   it   my   our
his   me   we   that   this   those   any   anyone
everything   mine   nobody   one   some   there

Paragraph 1 ....
Paragraph 2 ....
Paragraph 3 ....

We use pronouns in place of nouns. For example, here is a paragraph with no pronouns.

Mary went to the shops to buy apples. When Mary got to the shops Mary found the shops didn't have apples. So Mary went back home. When Mary got home, Mary saw there were apples in the fridge. Mary hadn't looked in the fridge before Mary went out.

Can you rewrite it, using the correct pronouns for the underlined words? Use the list above if you need some help.

Now read the text and answer questions 21–27.

PART 4

QUESTIONS 21–27

Read the article about some beautiful old cups.
Are sentences 21–27 'Right' (A) or 'Wrong' (B)?
If there is not enough information to answer 'Right' (A) or 'Wrong' (B), choose 'Doesn't say' (C).
For questions 21–27, mark A, B or C on your answer sheet.

The missing cups

When I was young, my parents moved from California to Illinois with me and my two sisters. We all helped my mother pack everything from our old house into boxes. Inside three of the boxes were my grandmother's special cups, bowls and plates. They were special because my grandmother, a clever artist, painted them herself with a lovely pattern of blue flowers.

Sadly, one of those three boxes was lost. We never got the cups, but the plates and bowls arrived safely. We used them on special days in the year, like birthdays. We remembered those cups and were sad that we did not have them any more.

Ten years later, I decided to go to university in California. In my first summer there, a friend asked me to spend the day at an antique market with her. At first, I didn't want to go, but I finally agreed and we had a great day there looking around. There were many old and interesting things for sale. We were just leaving when I saw a woman selling twelve beautiful cups with a pattern of blue flowers. I looked closely and saw they were my grandmother's cups!

Example:

0   The writer lived in California when she was a child.

    A Right   **B** Wrong   **C** Doesn't say   *Answer:*

0	A	B	C
	▬	▭	▭

---

21   The writer's grandmother asked an artist to paint the cups, plates and bowls for her.

    A Right   **B** Wrong   **C** Doesn't say

22   Some of the plates and bowls were broken when they arrived.

    A Right   **B** Wrong   **C** Doesn't say

23   The family forgot all about the grandmother's cups.

    A Right   **B** Wrong   **C** Doesn't say

24   The writer moved back to California because she wanted to study there.

    A Right   **B** Wrong   **C** Doesn't say

25   The writer went to the market alone in her first summer in California.

    A Right   **B** Wrong   **C** Doesn't say

26   The writer enjoyed looking at things for sale at the market.

    A Right   **B** Wrong   **C** Doesn't say

27   The writer paid a lot of money to buy the cups at the market.

    A Right   **B** Wrong   **C** Doesn't say

TIP

Check that the verbs, adjectives and pronouns fit with the tenses and nouns in the text.

Part 5 tests grammar. Here is a list of the grammar points tested in this text in Part 5.

conjunctions   articles   pronouns
past tense of verb 'to be'   adjectives
past tense of verb 'to carry'

Look at the text and questions 28–35 and the example. Decide which grammar point each question tests. You may want to use a learners' dictionary.

Now look at the article about ships and answer these questions.

1   What tense are the verbs in paragraphs 1, 2 and 3 in?

2   What tense are the verbs in the last paragraph in?

3   Which noun must the answer to question 28 go with: 'people', 'ships' or 'years'?

4   Which noun must the answer to question 30 go with: 'life', 'sailors' or 'journey'?

5   In the text around question 31, do the sailors have a lot of food or not a lot of food?

6   What does the pronoun 'these' after question 34 mean: 'times' or 'oil tankers'?

Now answer questions 28–35.

PART 5

Read the article about ships.
Choose the best word (A, B or C) for each space.
For questions 28–35, mark A, B or C on your answer sheet.

Ships – faster and bigger

The first people to build ships **(0)** ………… the Egyptians 5000 years ago. They used **(28)** ………… to travel on the River Nile, the longest river in Africa.

In the sixteenth century, people from Europe travelled thousands of kilometres in large ships. **(29)** ………… was important that they found new ways around the world. Life was hard for these sailors and on the journey **(30)** ………… died because they often didn't have **(31)** ………… food.

In the nineteenth century, ships called 'clippers' **(32)** ………… tea from China to Britain and wool from Australia to the USA. In very strong winds, clippers could sail 650 kilometres **(33)** ………… day.

In modern times, the largest ships are oil tankers. **(34)** ………… of these are 400 metres long **(35)** ………… the sailors have to use bicycles to travel round the ship!

Example:

0	**A** were	**B** are	**C** been	***Answer:***	0	A	B	C

28	**A** their	**B** them	**C** this

29	**A** There	**B** Here	**C** It

30	**A** many	**B** much	**C** more

31	**A** few	**B** enough	**C** little

32	**A** carried	**B** carrying	**C** carry

33	**A** the	**B** a	**C** one

34	**A** None	**B** Every	**C** Some

35	**A** so	**B** because	**C** when

TIP

Think about each description and what is being described.

Read the instructions. These are all words about things you can see in the countryside.

Are they going to be nouns, verbs or adjectives?

How do you know?

Look at the example. The important word here is 'animal'. This tells us what is being described. The rest of the information, 'eats grass ... make butter ... milk' just helps us decide what kind of animal it is – a cow.

Now look at sentences 36–40, and before you answer the question below, decide what is being described. Think about these questions: Is it a place, an object, an animal, or a building? How do you know? Is it singular or plural? How do you know?

Now answer questions 36–40.

Playing a game called 'Twenty Questions', with a friend or in your English class, can help you understand descriptions.

This is how you play the game. One person thinks of a noun or a verb. Now the other person or class can ask 20 'yes/no' questions to try to guess what the first person is thinking about.

For example:

1	Is it a noun?	Yes
2	Is it alive?	Yes
3	Is it a person?	No
4	Is it an animal?	Yes
5	Is it a pet?	No
6	Does it live on a farm?	No
7	Does it live in a zoo?	Yes
8	Is it dangerous?	Yes
9	Does it have big teeth?	Yes
10	Is it an orange-brown colour?	Yes
11	Is it from Africa?	Yes

What do you think it is? (Remember, you can ask nine more questions.)

PART 6

QUESTIONS 36–40

Read the descriptions of some things you can see in the countryside.
What is the word for each one?
The first letter is already there. There is one space for each other letter in the word.
For questions 36–40, write the words on your answer sheet.

Example:

0   This animal eats grass, and people make butter from its milk.   c _ _

	Answer:	**0**	cow

----

36   People live in this place but it is not as big as a town.   v _ _ _ _ _

37   It may be quite dark here because there are so many trees.   f _ _ _ _ _

38   You can walk up and down these and they are smaller than mountains.   h i l l s

39   There are thousands of different kinds of these and flies are one example.   i _ _ _ _ _ _

40   If there's a river, you'll need to walk over this to cross it.   b _ _ _ _ _

TIP

Always check your answers by reading the text again, with your answers in the spaces. Always be careful when you copy your answers onto the answer sheet.

Read the message put on the internet by Sara Lewis.

When you read it the first time, don't try to think of the words to go in the spaces, just try to understand the message.

Now read it a second time and answer questions 41–50.

Below are the answers a KET candidate put on their answer sheet.

Part 7		Do not write here
41	to	1 41 0
42	being	1 42 0
43	do	1 43 0
44	does	1 44 0
45	me	1 45 0
46	they	1 46 0
47	have	1 47 0
48	every	1 48 0
49	write	1 49 0
50	abowt	1 50 0

This candidate only got two marks for the answers to question 47 and 49, and no marks for all the other answers.

Here is a list of the problems the candidate had. Can you match the problems with the questions? (You may need to use some of the problems twice.) Write the question numbers in the boxes next to the problems.

writing the answer in the wrong place on the answer sheet	
using the right verb, but not making it fit with the subject of the sentence	
not reading and understanding the whole paragraph	
using the wrong spelling	
using the wrong preposition	
using the right verb, but the wrong form	

Now you have seen some of the problems candidates can have with this part of the test. Think of four things candidates should check when they are answering Part 7.

PART 7

QUESTIONS 41–50

Complete this message left on the Internet by Sara Lewis.
Write ONE word for each space.
For questions 41–50, write the words on your answer sheet.

Example:

0	years

My name is Sara Lewis and I am fourteen (0) .... old. I
live in the centre (41) .... Toronto, Canada. When I grow
up, I want to (42) .... an actress. My father (43) ....
not think this is a good idea! He is a doctor and he wants
(44) .... to study medicine at university. But I know I
won't like medicine. I have science lessons at school and
(45) .... are very boring.

I (46) .... like to travel all around the world. I (47) ....
only been to Europe once. We usually spend our holidays in
Canada but (48) .... year we may visit Australia. Please
(49) .... an email to tell me (50) .... your life.

TIP

Only write the information asked for on the form. Do not write any extra information.

Now answer questions 51–55.

When you have checked your answers, look at this candidate's answers. Is there anything wrong with them?

Look at the instructions, letter, note and booking form and try to answer these questions.

1 Who is Mr Taylor?

2 Who is Lois Jones?

3 Who is Suzanna?

4 Who will fill in the booking form?

Now look at the booking form.

Here is a list of the kind of information you often have to put on forms. Put a tick (✓) next to the information if it needs to be on the school trip booking form and a cross (✗) if it doesn't. The first one has been done for you.

Part 8		Do not write here
51	4A	1 51 0
52	Blackfort Castle or Walton Zoo	1 52 0
53	bus	1 53 0
54	6th	1 54 0
55	£10–£15	1 55 0

People's names ✓

Dates

Addresses

Times

Days of the week

Phone numbers

Prices

Names of places

Type of transport

PART 8

QUESTIONS 51–55

Read the letter and the note about a school trip.
Fill in the information on the School Trip Booking Form.
For questions 51–55, write the information on your answer sheet.

---

8 December

Dear Mr Taylor,

On 6th January there is a trip for classes 3A and 4A to Blackfort Castle or Walton Zoo. The cost is only £10 – last year it was £15!

We could go by train or by bus. Please tell us which you prefer by 15th December.

Lois Jones

Dad,

Please fill in my form. I don't want to visit a castle, but the zoo sounds great.

Remember, I'm not in 3A now!

I don't want to travel by bus – it takes too long!

Suzanna

School Trip Booking Form

Student's name: _Suzanna Taylor_

Class:	**51**	
Trip to:	**52**	
Travel by:	**53**	
Date of trip:	**54**	
Cost:	**55**	£

TIP

Read through your answer and make sure that it is long enough and has all three points.

Look at the instructions for this Part 9 test and answer these questions.

1 Who are you writing to?

2 Whose bedroom are you going to paint?

3 How long will your note be?

Now look at Tsin's note to Robbie. Remember the instructions for this task are 'say' not 'ask'.

> What colour paint use for bedroom? I prefer green, what time you start and what wear?
>
> Tsin

4 Does Tsin write about all three points in the correct way?

5 Is the note long enough?

Now look at Paul's note to Robbie.

6 Is this note better or worse than Tsin's note?

7 Has Paul given Robbie the three points of information?

8 Is Paul's note long enough?

> Hello Robbie,
>
> I think it's great to paint my bedroom in red or in green. I will start tomorrow at 9 o'clock, bring a T-shirt and a pair of jeans.
>
> See you tomorrow.
>
> Paul

PART 9

QUESTION 56

You are going to paint your bedroom. Your friend Robbie is going to help you.
Write a note to Robbie.

Say:

- what **colour** paint you are going to use

- what **time** you will start

- what **clothes** to wear.

Write 25–35 words.

Write the note on your answer sheet.

Listening ● PART 1

TIP

You will hear all three options, A, B and C, on the recording but only one is the correct answer. You need to read the questions carefully and make sure you answer the question.

Before you listen, look at questions 1–5 and answer these questions.

Question 1

What is Steve doing in each picture?

Question 2

What are the three types of transport?

Question 3

What are the three activities in the pictures?

Question 4

Where is the cat in each picture?

Question 5

What are the three jobs?

Now listen to the recording for question 1 only. You will hear all three activities from the pictures but only one is the activity that Steve is doing *now*. As you listen, answer these questions.

1 What does Steve's friend want Steve to do?

2 Where is Steve?

3 What will Steve do later in the afternoon?

For the right answer to question 1, 'What's Steve doing now?', you need to give the answer that shows what Steve is doing *now*, NOT what Steve's friend wants to do (picture A), NOT what Steve wants to do in the afternoon (picture B).

Now read the questions carefully. Then listen to the recording and answer questions 1–5.

PART 1

QUESTIONS 1–5

You will hear five short conversations.
You will hear each conversation twice.
There is one question for each conversation.
For questions 1–5, put a tick (✓) under the right answer.

Example:

0   How many people were at the meeting?

3	**13**	**30**
A ☐	B ☐	C ✓

1 What's Steve doing now?

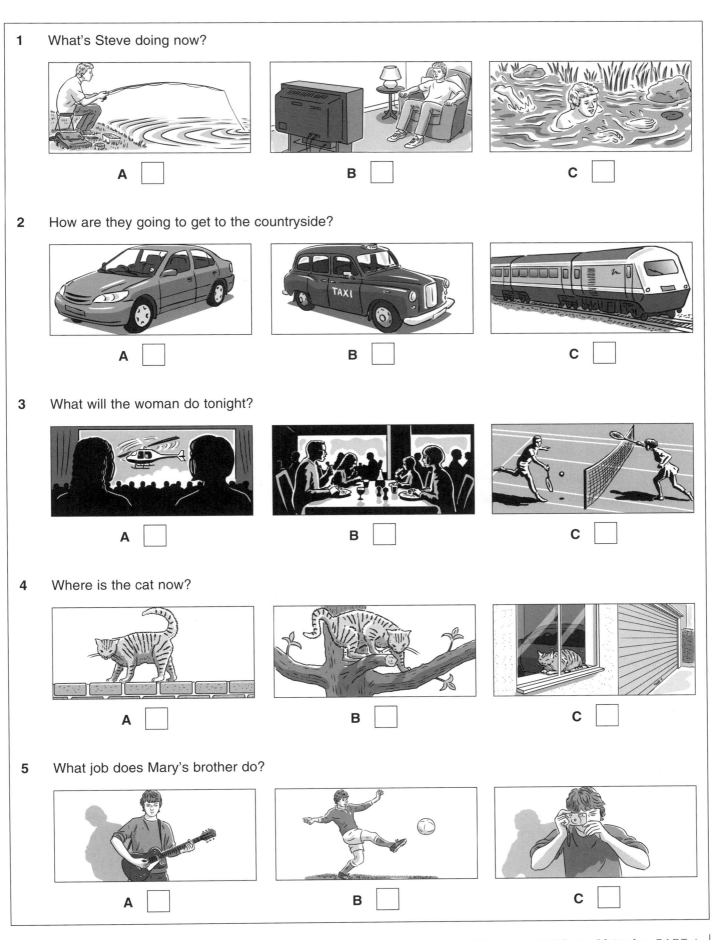

A ☐   B ☐   C ☐

2 How are they going to get to the countryside?

A ☐   B ☐   C ☐

3 What will the woman do tonight?

A ☐   B ☐   C ☐

4 Where is the cat now?

A ☐   B ☐   C ☐

5 What job does Mary's brother do?

A ☐   B ☐   C ☐

TIP

Check your answers when you listen for the second time. Remember you can only use an option once.

Before you listen, look at everything written on the question paper for this part.

1   What are the headings for the two lists, 6–10 and A–H?

2   Which letter, A–H, can you not use as an answer?

Listen to the recording once.

Now listen to the recording again and check these notes made by a candidate.

Question 6

Tuesday   E or H (science or tennis)

Question 7

Wednesday   ?

Question 8

Thursday   F (Spanish)

Question 9

Friday   D ? (piano)

Question 10

Saturday   G (swimming)

Did you help the candidate get the right answers?

PART 2

QUESTIONS 6–10

Listen to Jane telling her father about the extra subjects she is doing at school.
What subject does she do on each day?
For questions 6–10, write a letter A–H next to each day.
You will hear the conversation twice.

Example:

0   Monday   C

Days

6   Tuesday   ☐

7   Wednesday   ☐

8   Thursday   ☐

9   Friday   ☐

10   Saturday   ☐

Subjects

A   art

B   computer club

C   Japanese

D   piano

E   science

F   Spanish

G   swimming

H   tennis

All the answers to the questions will come from one person only in the conversation.

Look at the instructions, the example and the five questions, 11–15. Answer these questions.

1 Who is giving the answers in the conversation?

2 What is the conversation about?

The friend is asking Peter questions. Imagine you are Peter's friend. What questions could you ask him to get the answers to all the questions?

In the example, Peter says that he went to Durham on Friday. So the question must be, 'When did you go to Durham?'

Now think of all the questions you could ask Peter, to get the answers for questions 11–15.

Now listen to what Peter says on the recording and answer questions 11–15.

PART 3

QUESTIONS 11–15

Listen to Peter talking to a friend about a school trip.
For questions 11–15, tick (✓) A, B or C.
You will hear the conversation twice.

Example:

0 Peter went to Durham on
- **A** Wednesday. ☐
- **B** Thursday. ☐
- **C** Friday. ✓

---

11 The first place Peter visited was the
- **A** castle. ☐
- **B** museum. ☐
- **C** cathedral. ☐

12 Peter enjoyed listening to a talk about
- **A** paintings. ☐
- **B** stamps. ☐
- **C** clocks. ☐

13 Peter thought the castle was
- **A** empty. ☐
- **B** cold. ☐
- **C** dark. ☐

14 In a shop, Peter got
- **A** a book. ☐
- **B** some food. ☐
- **C** postcards. ☐

15 Peter took photographs of
- **A** windows. ☐
- **B** people. ☐
- **C** a bus. ☐

TIP

Practise saying the alphabet and listening to spellings and long numbers.

For questions 16–20, you may have to write down spellings or phone numbers that you hear in the recording.

Look at the notes about a theatre visit and decide what kind of information you will need to listen for to answer questions 16–20. Are you listening for numbers, times, dates, prices, ages or spellings of names or a word?

Before you listen to the recording, look at the list of surnames and phone numbers below. Practise reading these out so that someone else can write them down. Do not show the other person the names or numbers.

Greenwood 8855738   Dunmore 3992018
Plainer 9562224   Whitestone 1638264
Henderson 4728900

Sometimes in this part you will have to write a day of the week or a month of the year. Can you spell the days of the week and months? Do a quick spelling test now and write the 7 days and 12 months. Check your spellings in a dictionary.

Look at these names.

DESLAY TISELEY TISLIY DISLEY DESLIY

Practise saying the spellings of these names to yourself, out loud, letter by letter. For example, D – E – S – L – A – Y. Make sure you know the names of the vowel sounds A, E and I.

One of these names is the answer to question 18.

Now listen to the recording and answer questions 16–20.

PART 4

QUESTIONS 16–20

You will hear a telephone conversation about a show at a theatre.
Listen and complete questions 16–20.
You will hear the conversation twice.

THEATRE VISIT

Play:	Cinderella
There are tickets for:	**16** .... April
A child's ticket costs:	**17** £
Name of main actor:	**18** Sophie ....
Show begins at:	**19** .... p.m.
For information about Children's Club, phone	**20**

TIP

Use the information in the notes to help you.

Before you listen to the recording, look at the phone message. In the message, some information has already been filled in: 'Bike shop', '£', 'bicycle', 'p.m.' and 'King Street'.

This information and the prompts on the left of the notes can help you to find the information you need to answer questions 21–25.

Look at the notes and underline all the words that help you know what kind of information you need to listen for in questions 21–25.

Now listen to the recording and answer questions 21–25.

PART 5

QUESTIONS 21–25

You will hear a man leaving a message.
Listen and complete questions 21–25.
You will hear the information twice.

Phone Message

From:	Bike shop
Colour of bike:	**21**
Bike costs:	**22** £ ....
Shop has also got:	**23** bicycle ....
Come tonight before:	**24** .... p.m.
Address to go to:	**25** .... King Street

You now have 8 minutes to write your answers on the answer sheet.

The Speaking test lasts 8 to 10 minutes. You will take the test with another candidate. There are two examiners, but only one of them will talk to you. The examiner will ask you questions and ask you to talk to the other candidate.

Part 1 (5–6 minutes)
The examiner will ask you and your partner some questions. These questions will be about your daily life, past experience and future plans. For example, you may have to speak about your school, job, hobbies or home town.

Part 2 (3–4 minutes)
You and your partner will speak to each other. You will ask and answer questions. The examiner will give you a booklet with some information in it. The examiner will give your partner a booklet with some words in it. Your partner will use the words in the booklet to ask you questions about the information you have. Then you will change roles.

Speaking ● PART 1

TIP

Make sure you can talk about past, present and future events.

In the first part of the test the examiner will ask you questions about your daily life, past experiences and future plans.

Here are some examples of the kind of questions the examiner will ask you.

1 How much homework does your teacher give you?
2 What subjects did you study at school?
3 When will you go back to your country?
4 What did you do yesterday?
5 What will you do next weekend?
6 What do you like to read?

Which questions are about the past, which are about the present and which are about the future?

Practise answering these questions using the right tenses.

TIP

If you think your question is wrong, correct yourself by asking it again.

In the second part of the test the examiner wants to know if you can ask questions in English, using correct grammar.

Look at the information 4A on page 133. This is about maths lessons. There are also prompt questions 4B on page 131.

Look at 4B and then look at these questions.

1 When these maths lessons are?

2 What name of teacher?

3 Has teacher telephone number?

4 What cost maths lessons?

5 Where maths lessons?

All of these questions are grammatically wrong. In some, the word order is wrong; in others, there are words missing. Others use the wrong question word. Correct the sentences.

Now practise what to say when you correct yourself.

Here are some phrases you may want to use.

No, that's wrong. I'll say that again.

I mean …

I'll do that again.

Now, when you know your question is wrong, correct yourself and ask the right question. For example,

When these maths lessons are? I mean … when are the maths lessons?

Practise correcting yourself when you do the task about a school trip on pages 137 (4C) and 135 (4D).

Paper 3 frames

Tests 1–4

Part 1 (5–6 minutes)

Greetings and introductions

At the beginning of Part 1, the interlocutor greets the candidates, asks for their names and asks them to spell something.

Giving information about place of origin, occupation, studies

The interlocutor asks the candidates about where they come from/live, and for information about their school/studies/work.

Giving general information about self

The interlocutor asks the candidates questions about their daily life, past experience or future plans. They may be asked, for example, about their likes and dislikes, or about recent past experiences, or to describe and compare places.

Extended response

In the final section of Part 1, candidates are expected to give an extended response to a 'Tell me something about …' prompt. The topics are still of a personal and concrete nature. Candidates should produce at least three utterances in their extended response.

Test 1, Part 2 (3–4) minutes

Note: The visual materials for Part 2 appear on pages 130, 132, 134 and 136

The interlocutor introduces the activity as follows:

Interlocutor: *(Pablo)*, here is some information about a bird park.

(Interlocutor shows task 1A on page 130 to Pablo.)

(Laura), you don't know anything about the bird park, so ask *(Pablo)* some questions about it.

(Interlocutor shows task 1B on page 132 to Laura.)

Use these words to help you. *(Interlocutor indicates prompt words.)*

Do you understand?

Now, *(Laura)*, ask *(Pablo)* your questions about the bird park, and *(Pablo)*, you answer them.

When the candidates have asked and answered their questions about the bird park, they then exchange roles and talk about a different topic.

The interlocutor introduces the activity as follows:

Interlocutor: *(Laura)*, here is some information about an elephant ride.

(Interlocutor shows task 1C on page 134 to Laura.)

(Pablo), you don't know anything about the elephant ride, so ask *(Laura)* some questions about it.

(Interlocutor shows task 1D on page 136 to Pablo.)

Use these words to help you. *(Interlocutor indicates prompt words.)*

Do you understand?

Now, *(Pablo)*, ask *(Laura)* your questions about the elephant ride, and *(Laura)*, you answer them.

Note: Candidates are assessed on both their questions and answers in Part 2 of the test.

Test 2, Part 2 (3–4) minutes

Note: The visual materials for Part 2 appear on pages 130, 132, 134 and 136

The interlocutor introduces the activity as follows:

Interlocutor: *(Pablo)*, here is some information about some football lessons.

(Interlocutor shows task 2A on page 132 to Pablo.)

(Laura), you don't know anything about the football lessons, so ask *(Pablo)* some questions about them.

(Interlocutor shows task 2B on page 130 to Laura.)

Use these words to help you. *(Interlocutor indicates prompt words.)*

Do you understand?

Now, *(Laura)*, ask *(Pablo)* your questions about the football lessons, and *(Pablo)*, you answer them.

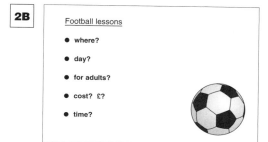

When the candidates have asked and answered their questions about the football lessons, they then exchange roles and talk about a different topic.

The interlocutor introduces the activity as follows:

Interlocutor: *(Laura)*, here is some information about a running race.

(Interlocutor shows task 2C on page 136 to Laura.)

(Pablo), you don't know anything about the running race, so ask *(Laura)* some questions about it.

(Interlocutor shows task 2D on page 134 to Pablo.)

Use these words to help you. *(Interlocutor indicates prompt words.)*

Do you understand?

Now, *(Pablo)*, ask *(Laura)* your questions about the running race, and *(Laura)*, you answer them.

Note: Candidates are assessed on both their questions and answers in Part 2 of the test.

Test 3, Part 2 (3–4) minutes

Note: The visual materials for Part 2 appear on pages 131, 133, 135 and 137

The interlocutor introduces the activity as follows:

Interlocutor: *(Pablo)*, here is some information about a sailing school.

(Interlocutor shows task 3A on page 131 to Pablo.)

(Laura), you don't know anything about the sailing school, so ask *(Pablo)* some questions about it.

(Interlocutor shows task 3B on page 133 to Laura.)

Use these words to help you. *(Interlocutor indicates prompt words.)*

Do you understand?

Now, *(Laura)*, ask *(Pablo)* your questions about the sailing school, and *(Pablo)*, you answer them.

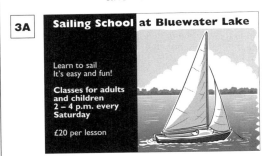

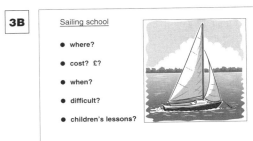

When the candidates have asked and answered their questions about the sailing school, they then exchange roles and talk about a different topic.

The interlocutor introduces the activity as follows:

Interlocutor: *(Laura)*, here is some information about a job advertisement.

(Interlocutor shows task 3C on page 135 to Laura.)

(Pablo), you don't know anything about the job advertisement, so ask *(Laura)* some questions about it.

(Interlocutor shows task 3D on page 137 to Pablo.)

Use these words to help you. *(Interlocutor indicates prompt words.)*

Do you understand?

Now, *(Pablo)*, ask *(Laura)* your questions about the job advertisement, and *(Laura)*, you answer them.

Note: Candidates are assessed on both their questions and answers in Part 2 of the test.

Test 4, Part 2 (3–4) minutes

Note: The visual materials for Part 2 appear on pages 131, 133, 135 and 137

The interlocutor introduces the activity as follows:

Interlocutor: *(Pablo)*, here is some information about a maths teacher.

(Interlocutor shows task 4A on page 133 to Pablo.)

(Laura), you don't know anything about the maths teacher, so ask *(Pablo)* some questions about him.

(Interlocutor shows task 4B on page 131 to Laura.)

Use these words to help you. *(Interlocutor indicates prompt words.)*

Do you understand?

Now, *(Laura)*, ask *(Pablo)* your questions about the maths teacher, and *(Pablo)*, you answer them.

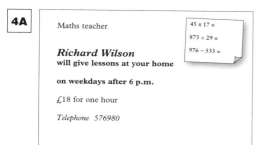

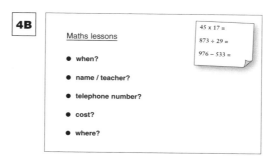

When the candidates have asked and answered their questions about the maths teacher, they then exchange roles and talk about a different topic.

The interlocutor introduces the activity as follows:

Interlocutor: *(Laura)*, here is some information about a school trip.

(Interlocutor shows task 4C on page 137 to Laura.)

(Pablo), you don't know anything about the school trip, so ask *(Laura)* some questions about it.

(Interlocutor shows task 4D on page 135 to Pablo.)

Use these words to help you. *(Interlocutor indicates prompt words.)*

Do you understand?

Now, *(Pablo)*, ask *(Laura)* your questions about the school trip, and *(Laura)*, you answer them.

Note: Candidates are assessed on both their questions and answers in Part 2 of the test.

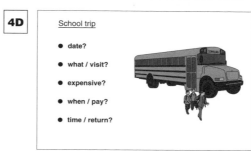

1A

Lightwood Bird Park

Look at beautiful birds from Europe, Africa and Asia

Learn how birds fly

February to December

10 a.m. – 5 p.m.

£2 children
£4 adults

Call 859261

2B

Football lessons

- **where?**

- **day?**

- **for adults?**

- **cost? £?**

- **time?**

3A

Sailing School at Bluewater Lake

Learn to sail
It's easy and fun!

**Classes for adults
and children
2 – 4 p.m. every
Saturday**

£20 per lesson

4B

Maths lessons

- **when?**

- **name / teacher?**

- **telephone number?**

- **cost?**

- **where?**

45 x 17 =

873 ÷ 29 =

976 – 533 =

1B

<u>Bird park</u>

- **what / see?**

- **open / February?**

- **what / learn?**

- **child's ticket? £?**

- **phone number?**

2A

FOOTBALL LESSONS

Tuesdays and Fridays

For players 12 – 16 years old

6 – 8 p.m.
£3 per lesson

**Must wear
football boots.**

NORTH ROAD SPORTS CENTRE

3B

Sailing school

- **where?**
- **cost? £?**
- **when?**
- **difficult?**
- **children's lessons?**

4A

Maths teacher

Richard Wilson
will give lessons at your home

on weekdays after 6 p.m.

£18 for one hour

Telephone 576980

45 × 17 =

873 ÷ 29 =

976 − 533 =

1C

Katie the Elephant!

You can ride an elephant
next Saturday
in **City Park**
£2

Safe for young children

Tel: 371294 to book

2D

Running race

- **where / start?**

- **long race?**

- **what / prize?**

- **date?**

- **more information?** ☎ **?**

3C

ARE YOU LOOKING FOR A JOB?

We need a Cook

July – September in the Park Hotel

25 hours per week

£6.40 per hour

Call 776 2143

4D

School trip

- **date?**

- **what / visit?**

- **expensive?**

- **when / pay?**

- **time / return?**

1D

Elephant ride

- **name / elephant?**

- **when / ride?**

- **price?   £?**

- **in zoo?**

- **dangerous?**

2C

Sunday 11th October at 9.00 a.m.

RUNNING RACE

10 kilometres

Starts: King's Bridge
Finishes: West Park

First Prize   £100

Phone Andy Smith: 683217

3D

Job

- where / job?
- what / job?
- how much / earn?
- hours per week?
- telephone number?

4C

School trip to

Science Museum

Wednesday 12th October

leave school   7.30 a.m.
return school   5.30 p.m.

£15 (with lunch in a restaurant)

Pay School Secretary by 30th September

Sample answer sheets

UNIVERSITY *of* **CAMBRIDGE**
ESOL Examinations

S A M P L E

Candidate Name
If not already printed, write name
in CAPITALS and complete the
Candidate No. grid (in pencil).

Candidate Signature

Examination Title

Centre

Supervisor:
If the candidate is ABSENT or has WITHDRAWN shade here ⊂⊃

Centre No.

Candidate No.

Examination Details

0	0	0	0
1	1	1	1
2	2	2	2
3	3	3	3
4	4	4	4
5	5	5	5
6	6	6	6
7	7	7	7
8	8	8	8
9	9	9	9

KET Paper 1 Reading and Writing Candidate Answer Sheet

Instructions

Use a PENCIL (B or HB).
Rub out any answer you want to change with an eraser.

For **Parts 1, 2, 3, 4** and **5**:
Mark ONE letter for each question.
For example, if you think **C** is the right answer to the
question, mark your answer sheet like this:

0   A B C

Part 1

1	A B C D E F G H
2	A B C D E F G H
3	A B C D E F G H
4	A B C D E F G H
5	A B C D E F G H

Part 2

6	A B C
7	A B C
8	A B C
9	A B C
10	A B C

Part 3

11	A B C
12	A B C
13	A B C
14	A B C
15	A B C

16	A B C D E F G H
17	A B C D E F G H
18	A B C D E F G H
19	A B C D E F G H
20	A B C D E F G H

Part 4

21	A B C
22	A B C
23	A B C
24	A B C
25	A B C
26	A B C
27	A B C

Part 5

28	A B C
29	A B C
30	A B C
31	A B C
32	A B C
33	A B C
34	A B C
35	A B C

Turn over for
Parts 6 – 9 →

For **Parts 6, 7 and 8:**

Write your answers in the spaces next to the numbers (36 to 55) like this:

0	example

Part 6

		Do not write here
36		1 36 0
37		1 37 0
38		1 38 0
39		1 39 0
40		1 40 0

Part 7

		Do not write here
41		1 41 0
42		1 42 0
43		1 43 0
44		1 44 0
45		1 45 0
46		1 46 0
47		1 47 0
48		1 48 0
49		1 49 0
50		1 50 0

Part 8

		Do not write here
51		1 51 0
52		1 52 0
53		1 53 0
54		1 54 0
55		1 55 0

Part 9 (Question 56): Write your answer below.

Do not write below (Examiner use only)

0	1	2	3	4	5

UNIVERSITY *of* CAMBRIDGE
ESOL Examinations

S A M P L E

Candidate Name
If not already printed, write name
in CAPITALS and complete the
Candidate No. grid (in pencil).

Candidate Signature

Examination Title

Centre

Supervisor:
If the candidate is ABSENT or has WITHDRAWN shade here ⬚

Centre No.

Candidate No.

Examination Details

0	0	0	0
1	1	1	1
2	2	2	2
3	3	3	3
4	4	4	4
5	5	5	5
6	6	6	6
7	7	7	7
8	8	8	8
9	9	9	9

KET Paper 2 Listening Candidate Answer Sheet

Instructions

Use a PENCIL (B or HB).

Rub out any answer you want to change with an eraser.

For **Parts 1, 2 and 3:**
Mark ONE letter for each question.
For example, if you think **C** is the right answer to the
question, mark your answer sheet like this:

0 | A B C

Part 1

1	A B C
2	A B C
3	A B C
4	A B C
5	A B C

Part 2

6	A B C D E F G H
7	A B C D E F G H
8	A B C D E F G H
9	A B C D E F G H
10	A B C D E F G H

Part 3

11	A B C
12	A B C
13	A B C
14	A B C
15	A B C

For **Parts 4** and **5:**
Write your answers in the spaces next to the
numbers (16 to 25) like this:

0 | example

Part 4

		Do not write here
16		1 16 0
17		1 17 0
18		1 18 0
19		1 19 0
20		1 20 0

Part 5

		Do not write here
21		1 21 0
22		1 22 0
23		1 23 0
24		1 24 0
25		1 25 0